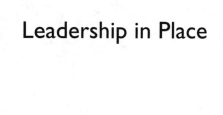

Leadership in Place

Leadership in Place

*How Academic Professionals
Can Find Their Leadership Voice*

Jon F. Wergin

Antioch University

EDITOR

ANKER PUBLISHING COMPANY, INC.
Bolton, Massachusetts

Leadership in Place
How Academic Professionals Can Find Their Leadership Voice

ISBN 978-1-933371-18-4

Composition by Julie Phinney
Cover design by Thomjon Borges

Anker Publishing Company, Inc.
563 Main Street
P.O. Box 249
Bolton, MA 01740-0249 USA

www.ankerpub.com

Library of Congress Cataloging-in-Publication Data
Wergin, Jon F.
Leadership in place : how academic professionals can find their
    leadership voice / Jon F. Wergin.
        p. cm.
 Includes bibliographical references and index.
        ISBN-13: 978-1-933371-18-4
    1. Universities and colleges—United States—Administration.
    2. Universities and colleges—United States—Faculty.
    3. Educational leadership—United States.   I. Title.

  LB2341.W437 2007
  378.1'01—dc22   2006032961

Table of Contents

About the Authors

Jon F. Wergin is professor of educational studies in the Ph.D. Program in Leadership and Change at Antioch University. He received his Ph.D. in educational psychology in 1973 from the University of Nebraska–Lincoln. For nearly 30 years he held faculty positions at Virginia Commonwealth University (VCU), serving in both administrative and faculty roles, and won awards for both teaching (1996) and scholarship (1998). As a faculty member in the School of Education he taught courses in adult and higher education and coordinated the Preparing Future Faculty for the Professions program through VCU's Graduate School. In 1992, he took a leave from VCU to be the founding director of the Forum on Faculty Roles and Rewards within the American Association for Higher Education (AAHE), and continued an active association with AAHE until its demise in 2004, focusing his scholarship on evaluation and change in academic departments. His monograph *The Collaborative Department* (1994) was the first published by AAHE under the auspices of the Forum. His other books and monographs include *Educating Professionals* (1993, with L. Curry), which won the Best Scholarly Publication award from Division I of the American Educational Research Association; *Analyzing Faculty Workload* (1994); *Analyzing and Evaluating Educational Research* (1996, 2001, and 2005, with J. McMillan); *and Departmental Assessment: How Some Campuses are Effectively Evaluating the Collective Work of Faculty* (AAHE, 2000, with J. N. Swingen), which reports the results of a national survey of departmental assessment practices for the Pew Charitable Trusts. He has also published numerous journal articles on such topics as professional education, assessment, and the restructuring of faculty work, including two articles in *Change* magazine on accreditation and student learning (2005). His most recent book *is Departments That Work: Creating and Sustaining Cultures of Excellence in Academic Departments* (Anker, 2003).

Dr. Wergin is past divisional vice president of the American Educational Research Association (Division I, Education in the Professions), and has served as chief evaluator of two national centers for research in higher education. In 2003 he completed work on a project funded by the Pew Charitable Trusts aimed at integrating efforts to assess student learning by the eight regional accrediting associations. He is a member of the National Academy for Higher Education Leadership, and has consulted with scores of national associations, accrediting bodies, and colleges and universities on issues related to evaluation and change in higher education.

The Contributors

Joseph Barwick is president of Carteret Community College. He has been in community college education most of his adult life and has enjoyed a variety of leadership positions in several organizations at the national, state, and local levels. His leadership interests include promoting workforce and economic development, and he has served as chair of the Chamber of Commerce and the Economic Development Council. On the national scene, he has served on the American Association of Community Colleges' Academic, Student, and Community Task Force, the Rural Community College Commission, and is presently the vice chair of the Executive Council of the Southern Association of Colleges and Schools' Commission on Colleges. He received his bachelor's and master's degrees from the University of North Carolina–Chapel Hill, and his Ph.D. from the University of Texas–Austin.

Ellen Russell Beatty is associate vice president for academic affairs at Southern Connecticut State University (SCSU). She has served as interim academic vice president with responsibility for the School of Business, dean of health and human services, and director of faculty development, all at SCSU. Dr. Beatty holds the rank of tenured professor of nursing. She earned a doctorate in education and a master's in education from Columbia University, as well as a master of arts degree from New York University. Dr. Beatty has extensive administrative experience in higher education including strategic planning, accreditation, assessment and planning, and budgetary allocation. She is currently a site visitor for the New England Association of Schools and Colleges.

Shelley A. Chapman is a Ph.D. candidate in the Leadership and Change in the Professions Program at Antioch University. Her research focuses on integrating transformative learning theory, adaptive leadership theory, and deliberative curriculum theory. She has been at Johns Hopkins University since 2000 where she is director of the Center for Teaching and Learning. In her role as director, she assists faculty in designing and redesigning academic programs to transform graduate professional education. She is also an instructor, teaching in the Graduate Certificate Programs for Adult Learning and for Business Leaders of Independent Schools, as well as graduate courses in ethics for business students. As a consultant, she works with colleges and universities to design and redesign programs. She earned a master's degree in instructional systems design from the University of Maryland and a master's degree in religious education from Wesley Biblical Seminary.

Victoria Hardy is academic department head of design and facilities at Wentworth Institute of Technology. Prior to her academic career, which also included 10 years of teaching, she spent 20 years managing facilities and consulting in the arts and entertainment industry. She is the author of the first edition of *The Fit Facility: Human and Environmental Factors in Facility Management,* published by the International Facility Management Association, and the contributing writer of *Module Eight: Facility Management* in the new fifth edition of the *Project Resource Manual* published by the Construction Specifications Institute. She was named the International Facility Management Association Distinguished Member of the Year for 2005 and was selected in 2001 as the Distinguished Educator. She holds a bachelor's degree from the University of Missouri, a master's degree in management from Aquinas College, and was a selected participant in the Stanford University Management Development Program.

Shana Hormann is director of the Center for Creative Change at Antioch University Seattle and core faculty for the graduate program in organizational psychology. She has been an affiliate associate professor at the University of Washington School of Social Work since 1994 and taught for the University of Alaska–Southeast in Juneau from 1981 to 1991. Prior to her role at Antioch she was an administrator for the Washington State Department of Social and Health Services Echo Glen Children's Center, a juvenile rehabilitation administration facility for adjudicated youth. She has worked both in Seattle and Juneau for sexual assault and domestic violence service centers. She is passionate about resolving organizational trauma and strengthening resilience in organizations that provide services to victims of trauma. She has trained law enforcement officials, social service professionals, clergy and lay people, school personnel, judges, and parents throughout the U.S. and Canada in organizational trauma, sexual assault, family violence, and juvenile offenders. She is currently a doctoral student in Antioch University's Ph.D. Program in Leadership and Change.

Mark Hower has been interim president of Antioch University Seattle since June 2006. Prior to this appointment, he served for three years as special assistant to the president, where he oversaw both outcomes assessment and planning and the budget process for the campus. He continued to teach as a visiting faculty member in the Center for Creative Change until December 2005, primarily in courses related to leadership and systemic change. He has extensive experience with the U.S. Peace Corps in a variety of roles, including country director in Tonga, South Pacific; desk officer responsible for establishing programs in Russia, Ukraine, and the Baltic States; and volunteer in Sierra Leone, West Africa. He has worked as a management and organizational change consultant and is currently a doctoral student in Antioch University's Ph.D. Program in Leadership and Change.

Susanne Morgan has taught in the Department of Sociology at Ithaca College since 1983, and in multiple institutions before that since 1972. As a leader in place, she has served Ithaca College as a department chair, coordinator of the Humanities and Sciences First-Year Seminar Program, and, since 2001, as coordinator of faculty development activities. In that half-time role she created the Center for Faculty Excellence which includes a group-based all-college mentoring program, an annual weeklong summer institute, a web-based resource, frequent talks, workshops, and discussions, and other resources for faculty members. An accomplished workshop leader, she has designed learning experiences for people inside and outside academia on topics including women's health and sexuality, AIDS awareness, welcoming diversity, using technology to transform teaching, and integrating data analysis across the curriculum.

As a change agent she has worked on issues of midlife and aging, lesbian and gay concerns, and dogs and community. Among the highlights of her current position is helping sociology students accomplish outstanding research projects while at the same time helping new and experienced faculty members accomplish outstanding teaching and scholarship.

Robert Page is associate professor of management at Southern Connecticut State University, where he specializes in entrepreneurship, organizational change, and international management. Dr. Page earned his Ph.D. in business administration, specializing in organizational theory, from the University of California–Irvine, his master's in organizational behavior at Brigham Young University, and his bachelor's in industrial and labor relations at Cornell University. He has served as co-chair of the General Education Review Taskforce and is a member of the National and Eastern Academies of Management, the Association of American Colleges and Universities, the International Academy of Business Disciplines, and the New England Business Administration Association.

"Professor X" is an associate professor at a research university.

Linda M. Randall is associate professor and associate provost at the University of Baltimore. She has led several leadership positions in higher education that have informed her leadership style. Dr. Randall has instituted a number of change initiatives at the department and university levels at several institutions of higher education, and in the course of those initiatives she has been able to garner strong participant support. She earned her master's degree at the Harvard Graduate School of Business and her doctorate in management at the University of Massachusetts–Amherst.

Carol A. Reineck is associate professor in the School of
Nursing at the University of Texas Health Science Center at San Antonio (UTHSCSA). She is associate scientist
for nursing research at the Regional Center for Health
Workforce Studies at UTHSCSA. At the time of this writing, she was interim chair of the Department of Family
Nursing Care. Dr. Reineck teaches graduate courses in
the nursing administration major, including organizational behavior and healthcare financial management.
She transitioned from 31 years of military leadership and
service in 2001. Her final position as a colonel was as
chief nurse executive of the worldwide U.S. Army Medical Command. Dr. Reineck earned her doctorate from
the University of Maryland in 1990. She has published
three book chapters, nineteen articles, five technical
reports, three research education workbooks, and developed a web site to disseminate her readiness research.
She was principal investigator on a clinical research
study and two congressionally funded studies on readiness to practice nursing in austere environments. She is
board certified in critical care nursing, advanced nursing administration, and online teaching. Dr. Reineck is
the recipient of the 1992 Surgeon General's U.S. Army
Nurse of the Year Award, a 1998 Johnson & Johnson/
Wharton School of Business Fellow, the 2003 McKevitt
Faculty Research Award, a 2004 Visiting Scholar, and
the 2004 Award for Exceptional Graduate Teaching from
UTHSCSA. An elected member of the national board of
directors for the American Organization of Nurse Executives, she serves on the faculty of the Aspiring Nurse
Leaders Institute.

Willis M. Watt is professor of speech communication and
dean of the School of Information and Technology at
Methodist College. Dr. Watt teaches a variety of courses
including conflict management, listening, persuasion,
business and professional speaking, and various lead-

ership courses. He earned his doctorate from Kansas State University in 1980. In 1996 he was selected by the Kansas Speech Communication Association as the Outstanding College Teacher of the Year. He was inducted into the Mid-America Education Hall of Fame in 1998. Dr. Watt has presented more than 50 scholarly papers at state, regional, national, and international conferences, with many of the papers being included in subsequent conference proceedings. He has authored or coauthored five books in the field of speech communication and business/professional speaking, several monographs about theatre, and coauthored a book chapter on intercollegiate debate. His writing includes a variety of poems published locally, nationally, and internationally. Dr. Watt is currently a copy and a review editor for the *Journal of Leadership Education*. He serves as a member of the Institute for Community Leadership, which provides a no-cost leadership development and training program to citizens of Cumberland County, North Carolina.

Foreword

Colleges and universities have presented leadership conundrums to generations of administrators, faculty, board members, and writers and thinkers from the most varied perspectives. One contrasts the personal memoirs of Ivy League institution presidents and provosts, including Harold Dodds, Henry Wriston, Henry Rosovsky, and Derek Bok, with the more theoretical contributions of Michael Cohen and James March, Robert Birnbaum, and J. Victor Baldridge. Pragmatists like Allan Tucker have written extensively from their experiences in a variety of positions as well. Some have presented jaded views of the academic organization, such as Warren Bennis's *Why Leaders Can't Lead* (Jossey-Bass, 1997) and George Keller's *Academic Strategy* (The Johns Hopkins University Press, 1983), both of which lamented the intractability of academic culture and its imperviousness to leadership and change. The field does not want for prescriptions, conceptualizations, and exhortations.

Yet this vast trove of purported wisdom remains somehow unsatisfying and desperately random. How does one make sense of it? How would one integrate it to draw a coherent cognitive map to help leaders lead?

Jon Wergin, whose grounding is in psychology and who has long experience in higher education, has taken a new and different approach in this book. Assertively non-Olympian in its origins, this book builds on the lived experiences and earned insights of "regular" academic leaders—people around whose stories this book is constructed, people who have learned from doing. But their varied chapters also establish them as reflective thinkers who are literate in contemporary thought about leadership. It is a ranging and stimulating set of reflections, tied together insightfully in a final chapter by Wergin himself.

Wergin opens the book with a clear statement of what is at stake. In a time of increasing calls for accountability from many fronts, faculty at the nation's colleges and universities appear to have pulled back from constructive partnership in the enterprise, seeing their own careers and programs as the focus of their principal efforts—a trend newly confirmed by Jack Schuster and Martin Finkelstein in their analysis of national data on faculty work and careers.

This apparent abandonment of community threatens the academy in many ways, but most seriously at its core: the integrity of academic programs. Several decades ago, Martin Trow, a University of California sociologist, foresaw the effects of professionalization among faculty, pointing out that they would be drawn more and more into the orbits and communities of their disparate disciplines and away from engagement in their host universities. This "centrifugal force," he suggested, could have a malign effect—precisely Wergin's worry and his motive for this book.

Wergin and the book's chapter authors start from the premise that the public wants colleges and universities to be effectively led and accountable for student learning, growth, and development. Who should lead colleges and universities and how they should lead has remained a source of ambivalence and frustration as the academic community has become more fragmented amidst decades of growth and change. Culturally, positional leaders enjoy presumptive legitimacy. But that legitimacy is fragile in organizations that employ autonomous professionals such as faculty. The premise of this book is that colleges and universities may be effectively led by emergent acts of leadership from anyone who chooses to lead, a line of thought that has been developed in the more progressive contemporary studies of leadership. How does emergent or in-place leadership work? How do we know it when we experience it? Is it effective? Why? Or why not? These are the central questions that have engaged the book's authors, and that will engage the reader.

This book is based on the varied experience of the authors, who bring different intellectual perspectives to their interpretations of leadership. They are candid, reflective, and openly autobiographical. They demonstrate a deep regard for the humanity of their colleagues and their work. But they all wrestle with their understanding of what it takes to bring people together in service to organizational change. Their stories enrich the reader's understanding.

In-place leadership is emergent. It springs from the soil, so to speak. It is not a quality of people, nor a perquisite of position, but is instead a quality of behavior that compels others to pay attention, to see things anew, and to join forces in a common cause. It is neither permanent, nor is it always wholly successful. But it brings honesty, sincerity, openness, and transparency to a challenge. It fosters mutuality and trust, because it is based not on power, but on deeply human exchange (Who are we? What should we do?). It is not founded in naïveté, however. These chapters bring home the degree to which in-place leaders can act one step removed from the fray, planning and framing their own actions through "meta-leadership" that consciously brings others into the process and spreads ownership for solutions.

The book's chapter authors show a strong awareness of organizational psychodynamics, the ways in which people's needs and aspirations drive them, and of the cultures—both organizational and professional—in which faculty values are rooted. In some cases, the authors found themselves thrown into situations for which they had no formal preparation, but all had enough intuitive insights into how and why people behave as they do and enough conceptual sophistication to succeed as emergent leaders themselves. They came away with important insights to share.

This book never takes on the hectoring tone of spuriously convinced "gurus." Instead, the authors honor the reality of imperfect people grappling with difficult problems in imperfect institutions. They accept the need for trial and error learning, and they understand that their own leadership episodes are transient in the longer history of their colleges and universities.

This "grounded definition . . . [of] what leaders do and how they do it," as Wergin notes in his concluding chapter, is a valuable and realistic compendium from which anyone who might "emerge" can learn. I came away from reading this book feeling that even I might occasionally find the courage to move my colleagues, my department, and my institution in the kind of subterranean yet supremely conscious ways these successful in-place leaders have done. It is a message that will help academics justify reengagement and recommitment to their institutions and to the good to which they instinctively know they should be dedicated.

David W. Leslie
Chancellor Professor of Education
The College of William and Mary

1

Why We Need Leadership in Place

Jon F. Wergin

Suggest to a typical faculty member that "academic leadership is everybody's business," and you'll likely get a response like one of the following:

"Right. Tell that to the president."

"What? And put all those high-priced administrators out of work?"

"Not me. I don't have enough time for my *own* work, let alone somebody else's."

In other words, faculty and other academic staff don't have the power, the inclination, or the time to be leaders. It wasn't always this way. Leadership in place is an old idea, dating back more than a century, when what Bergquist (1992) has called the "collegial culture" first took root in the United States. In the collegial culture, a hybrid of the British and German models of higher education, faculty members were highly autonomous professionals with a great distrust of formal authority. If they deigned to be "led" at all it was by a charismatic fellow academic with whom they could identify. The business of running the campus was therefore something that everybody did, largely through the give-and-take politics of campus committees. The good faculty member was thus also a good university "citizen" (Rosovsky, 1990).

The collegial culture has been much maligned for its insularity, clubbiness, and resistance to change—and much of the criticism is well deserved. In the collegial culture, it's all about the faculty and their interests. John Millet (1962) captured the sentiment of the collegial culture this way:

> The key element in the academic process and in the academic community is the faculty. There is no other justification for the existence of a college or a university except to enable the faculty to carry on its instructional and research activities. Without a faculty higher education has no reason for being. (p. 65)

One doesn't have to be terribly close to the higher education scene to recognize that while some vestigial elements of the collegial culture are left in many modern universities, especially the elite ones, the image of the academy as a traditional collegium exists today only in fancy. Colleges and universities have become far different institutions and are now led in significantly different ways. There are many reasons for this, most of which center on the accountability movement that swept the country back in the 1980s and infiltrated even the previously impermeable walls of academe. "To whom is higher education responsible, for what purposes, for whose benefit, by which means, and with what consequences?" (Burke & Associates, 2005, p. x). Questions like these, asked routinely these days, were unheard of in the mid-20th century, because the answers were simple and obvious: Society's interests are served by advancing the faculty's interests. Academic quality is what faculty say it is; they are the experts on such matters after all. Just don't expect them to tell you how they know it or why they know it.

The public isn't buying this anymore. According to Joseph Burke and Associates (2005), two developments have driven the push for greater public accountability by colleges and universities, namely, "the mass movement of postsecondary education from the private privilege of the favored few to the public right of most Americans," and "the growing public perception that higher education has become the source of success for states and individuals in a knowledge and information era" (p. xi). In other words, now that college is for everyone, not just an elite few, and because it serves a key role in economic mobility and success, higher education must be able to demonstrate its contributions to the public good.

The insular world of the traditional collegium isn't prepared to deal with public accountability. And so a competing culture has grown up around it, sometimes displacing it entirely. This has been variously called the "bureaucratic institution" (Birnbaum, 1988), the "managerial culture" (Bergquist, 1992), and the "corporate university" (Levine, 2000). The reader can easily imagine the commonalities among these terms: clearly distinct administrative and professional functions, elaborate organizational charts and reporting structures, and codified procedures and regulations, all designed to address the demands placed on the institution by its various constituencies. The academic bureaucracy has grown so large at many universities that it has become what Zemsky and Massy (1993) have called an "administrative lattice," threatening to smother the core academic functions of teaching, research, and service.

This new academic bureaucracy holds little appeal for most faculty, who were attracted to the academy in the first place primarily on the basis of its promise of professional autonomy and academic community (Wergin, 2001). Why should they want to become part of a world they thought they had successfully avoided, a rather cold and intellectually empty place?

And what of the traditional forms of collegial leadership, such as academic committees and faculty senates? With a few exceptions—mostly elite universities with powerful faculty and a strong sense of tradition—these

functions have devolved into advisory capacities. Most
faculty senates are no longer true legislative bodies but
rather forums for disgruntled faculty to air their griev-
ances. Politics and economics dictate whether the central administration pays any attention or not. Election to
the senate, and to other forms of shared governance like
curriculum committees, is less an honor than a duty to
be undertaken reluctantly. "Why bother? The real decisions are made elsewhere anyway."

And so what has evolved is an ever-widening gulf
between faculty members and the administration of the
institution. Faculty who aspire to leadership roles have to
contend with the skepticism and sometimes even derision
of their peers. They are described as "crossing over" to
administration. They are assumed to have venal motives,
such as the desire for a larger office, a full-time assistant,
and a higher salary. They are assumed to be power hun-
gry. And most psychologically damaging, aspiring academic leaders have to live with the suspicion by others
that they want a leadership position, because they can't
cut it doing teaching or research. It's a wonder that we
have as many talented academic leaders as we do.

Unfortunately for the academy, several forces threaten
to make the gulf between academic workers and their
formal leadership even wider. The reluctance by most
faculty members to search out leadership roles has been
reinforced by a faculty reward system that is notoriously
out of whack with Rosovsky's (1990) notion of the "university citizens" faculty should aspire to be. Especially
at research universities, but also at comprehensive universities and even liberal arts colleges, faculty members
are rewarded for their scholarship first, teaching second, and service (including service to the institution) a
distant third (Fairweather, 1996). The more productive
one's scholarship, especially via single-authored articles
in refereed journals, and the more research grants one
pulls in, the higher the salary and professional prestige;

the more one focuses on teaching and service, the lower one's salary and prestige.

   In summary, economic and political forces for greater social accountability have forced colleges and universities to create more bureaucratic governance structures, which serve to distance faculty and other academic professionals from key decision-making roles. Faculty have widened this fissure by becoming more atomized and specialized in the work they do, and by clinging to a reward system that encourages individual scholarly productivity at the expense of contributions to the institution. Finally, and most perversely, the institution's formal leadership itself reinforces all of this by engaging in "mission creep": creating various initiatives intended to enhance the institution's prestige, generally by encouraging more funded research and Ph.D. production.

Forces for Change

It's time we rethink how our colleges and universities are organized and led. Transformative change is coming, and in some ways is already here. While political pressure for greater accountability has been the chief catalyst for change, other forces for change have huge implications for academic leadership.

Changes in the Faculty Workforce

A huge and potentially positive force for change lies within the faculty population itself. By 2010 higher education will experience the greatest faculty turnover in more than 30 years, due both to retirements of the large numbers of faculty members hired in the 1960s boom and to the hiring of new faculty to meet the enrollment crunch. The California State University System has estimated the equivalent of 100% turnover of faculty between 2000 and 2010. The turnover will be more than just in numbers; two other significant trends are upon us. First, we are witnessing a generational shift among new faculty, who as a group are significantly less willing than their elders to sacrifice their personal lives in the pursuit of tenure. These new faculty, increasingly female (nearly half of all new hires) and more ethnically diverse, are demanding a workplace that supports a more integrated lifestyle. These new faculty see themselves more often as independent agents, not tied to a particular institution, but rather to a set of more personal criteria, such as location and career flexibility. Second, an astonishing percentage of new full-time faculty, more than half and increasing, are being hired into nontenure-track appointments and devote a much greater proportion of their time to teaching. The huge bulge of faculty members hired in the 1960s and early 1970s now nearing retirement age will only accelerate these trends.

Expansion of the Definition of "Faculty"

Traditionally, the roles of faculty members and other academic staff have been quite distinct. Faculty spend most of their time preparing for and delivering classroom instruction and doing scholarship, while students spend much of *their* time interacting with librarians, information technologists, and student affairs staff, all professionals who are typically not well integrated into the educational delivery system.

These distinctions are becoming blurry. Librarians and student affairs staff have been redefining their academic roles for several years. In the late 1990s the Association of College and Research Libraries (ACRL) published a report stating that the academic work of librarians corresponded to Boyer's four categories of scholarship: inquiry, integration, application, and pedagogy of teaching (American Library Association, 1998). In 2002 the ACRL identified seven top issues facing academic libraries, one of which was the "role of the library in the academic enterprise" as a "place of intellectual stimulation and a center of activity on campus" (Hisle, 2002, ¶ 5).

Student affairs professionals are redefining their roles in more traditionally academic terms, as well. *Learning Reconsidered* (Keeling, 2004), a joint publication of the National Association of Student Personnel Administrators (NASPA) and the American College Personnel Association (ACPA), argues for the "integrated use of all of higher education's resources in the education and preparation of the whole student" (p. 1). The publication reexamines "widely accepted ideas about conventional teaching and learning, and [questions] whether current organizational patterns in higher education support student learning and development in today's environment" (Keeling, 2004, p. 1).

More active faculty-like roles taken on by professional library and student affairs staff will require a level of collaboration not seen before. Traditionally, faculty members use academic staff largely as consultants and sources of information, but rarely as partners in framing the educational process itself. As long as faculty and academic staff are physically separated, these traditional patterns will likely continue. Studies of partnerships between faculty members and other academic staff indicate that such partnerships are fragile and mostly ad hoc. They are sustained only when two conditions are met (Cook-Sather, 2001):

- The institution creates shared space and opportunities for serendipitous encounters and informal conversation.
- Faculty and their academic partners are mutually respectful, and all are willing to relinquish some professional autonomy. Academic staff are invited into conversations about scholarship, and faculty are invited into conversations about information acquisition and student development.

In the traditional academic organization, roles are scripted according to preconceptions about power and status. Library and student affairs staff are there to serve the faculty in a relationship that is primarily contractual. Colleges and universities working seriously on the integration of professional roles have found that a necessary condition for this reconfiguration is a setting in which professors, librarians, and student affairs staff are invited to participate on an equal footing. In this setting they are free to clarify their understanding of their own and others' roles, to imagine and pursue different possibilities, and to discover points of connection.

Democratization of Student Access

College enrollment during the next decade will increase by more than 3 million students, mostly from formerly underrepresented groups. Whereas having a college degree once was considered to be a sufficient but not necessary condition for moving up the economic ladder, the situation is reversed today. Higher education is considered necessary for economic success, but insufficient to guarantee it. Students are therefore more "instrumental" than they used to be, yet less interested in the college experience than in gaining a competitive edge in the marketplace. Social pressure to be college educated will increase. Already, there is broad agreement that a high school diploma has been replaced by at least two years of postsecondary education as the minimum education credential. Pressure for better student academic support will increase apace, but without commensurate financial support to institutions, resulting in pressure on them to deliver education more cost effectively.

The Digital Revolution

The influence of technology has garnered more ink among higher education pundits than any other force for change. Some recent essays, with their grim warnings about how traditional higher education risks having its core functions usurped by high-tech providers of web-based learning, border on the hysterical. At the same time such respected authorities as Robert Zemsky and William Massy (2004) have concluded that distance learning doesn't deserve all the hype—that while it could have significant payoff in student learning if well conceived and utilized, performance to date has fallen well short of early promises.

Nonetheless, it's clear that technology is forcing major changes in educational delivery. Online digital technology has weakened traditional geographic student catchment areas, resulting in an academic free-for-all, with dozens of institutions entering the academic marketplace and advertising online degrees that can be earned largely at home. This competition has spawned an increasing number of cooperative agreements between public and private programs and mergers between institutions hoping to reduce operating costs. In addition, the for-profit sector is, not surprisingly, going after the traditional "cash cows" of institutions, their undergraduate and graduate programs in business and management, a strategy that has already resulted in income and budget shortfalls.

The Democratization of Knowledge

The technological revolution is part of, and has contributed to, a larger and more powerful cultural transformation. Colleges and universities once were elite repositories of knowledge; they were places where people went to partake of erudition and specialized expertise, and where professors "professed." Because of the GI Bill and the Civil Rights Act, the last 50 years have witnessed an enormous change in access to the academy, making the elite available to nearly everyone. Today the nearly 3,500 institutions of higher education in the U.S. are geographically accessible to more than 90% of the population. In the past few years this democratization of access has been joined by the democratization of information: The explosive growth of technology has made the traditional notion of the academic library as a strictly physical place all but obsolete. Thus, libraries, and the universities that house them, are increasingly becoming virtual spaces.

The crumbling of physical boundaries between the campus and the community has led to a proliferation of other players in the knowledge business. These other players include not just proprietary colleges, such as the University of Phoenix, but also museums, public libraries, and corporations, more than 1,000 of which have "corporate universities," each engaged in the business of educating the company's workforce.

In summary, massive changes are under way in who the faculty are and how they work. These changes also raise fresh questions about the very nature of higher education as a social institution: If colleges and universities are not the elite fonts of knowledge that they used to be, then what are they for? What social purpose should they serve? And if the principal reason for having faculty members is no longer to maintain, control, and profess the knowledge base, then what social purpose should *faculty* serve? The isolation of the academy from public scrutiny is gone forever, and that's a good thing. However we cannot delude ourselves into thinking that some form of the bureaucratic/managerial culture will give us the academy we need. *Bureaucracies resist change, even when change is needed.* And when they do change, they create more complex structures rather than refine and simplify old ones. Peter Block (1995), organizational consultant to industry, government, and education, put it this way:

> The [bureaucratic] model is designed for the convenience of the supplier. It is organized for the sake of consistency, control, and predictability and is successful when the institution has little

real competition and is relatively wealthy. This strategy works when the institution is in control of the relationship with the customer . . . The problem is that colleges and universities no longer control their customers. (p. 8)

The predominant models of academic organization, especially the isolation of individual faculty members brought on by their highly specialized work, has produced a culture in which little collective responsibility to the institution exists. As long as faculty maintain strong ties to their academic disciplines, teach their own courses satisfactorily, and serve on an occasional campus committee, the collective good of the institution can be someone else's problem—just as assembly-line workers feel no collective responsibility for the cars they're making, only for the doors they're putting on. But unlike the factory worker, college faculty also run the assembly line. Such a system discourages new ways of thinking about the whole and virtually guarantees trouble for the new president or provost who wants to engage in institutional "transformation." This is not the fault of the faculty, as they are only doing what the institution is rewarding them for. The problem lies with an academic organization that no longer works.

Clinging to a managerial culture and its insistence on stability, predictability, and control and, therefore, its built-in resistance to change, would mean doing more of what we are already doing: making faculty work more specialized, creating more centers and institutes to meet external demands for interdisciplinary work and community engagement, enlarging the administrative lattice to coordinate all of this, and devoting a huge amount of energy to generate income sufficient to keep the whole machine running. Hanging on in this way will, according to the Project for the Future of Higher Education (Guskin & Marcy, 2003), result in more cuts and layoffs, more pressure to hire inexpensive faculty into nontenure-track positions, a heavier faculty workload, and higher student tuition.

Types of Leadership

We need a different form of leadership, one that encourages academic professionals to participate more effectively in reframing and rebuilding the changing social covenant of the academy, one that will begin to bridge the gulf between faculty and administration that has become so toxic under the managerial culture. We need a return to the old collegial model but with a modern twist, a sort of neocollegial model that engages faculty members and other academic professionals in the life of the campus while forswearing the clubbiness and insularity of the past. In a sense this is not a new model at all but rather a shift in attitude about leaders and leadership—from a hierarchical view that academic leadership flows from a leadership *position*, to a much more lateral view that leadership roles are available to everyone. This reconfiguration would be one that does, in fact, make leadership everybody's business.

Posthierarchical notions of leadership are relatively recent, having appeared in the general management literature only since the mid 1970s. Two seminal works in that decade started the trend, and many others have followed.

The better known of these is James MacGregor Burns's (1978) book on "transformative leadership." Burns was among the first to describe the shift from a "command-and-control" vision of leadership to one that is more inclusive and participatory. Burns's original thesis was that by focusing on shared goals and values, leaders and followers would raise one another to higher levels of motivation and morality and thus engage in a conscious transformation process. The problem with adapting Burns's ideas for academic leadership is that he presumes that leaders have some position of formal authority; thus the energy for transformation has a slightly patronizing air to it, even a bit of cultural imperialism. (Many campus leaders have, in fact, hijacked Burns's term and used it in ways he never intended, namely to transform a campus in a mostly unilateral fashion.)

The other big idea from the late 1970s, one that has gained momentum in recent years, is "servant leadership" (Greenleaf, 1977). Greenleaf's vision was much like Burns's except that he focused even more on the emancipatory needs of followers. His view was that leadership should at its core attend to matters of inequality and social injustice. Servant leadership has influenced many thinkers, writers, and social leaders, but for most people it has been more of a guiding philosophy than a guide to practice. Barbuto and Wheeler (2005) undertook a comprehensive literature review of servant leadership, identified 11 core characteristics, and then through factor analysis identified five core qualities: *altruistic calling*, "a leader's deep-rooted desire to make a positive difference in others' lives"; *emotional healing*, "a leader's commitment to and skill in fostering spiritual recovery from hardship or trauma"; *wisdom*, "a combination of awareness of surroundings and anticipation of consequences"; *persuasive mapping*, "influencing others using sound reasoning and mental frameworks"; and *organizational stewardship*, "preparing an organization to leave a positive legacy" (p. 23).

Aside from some experimentation with servant-leadership structures in community colleges (Smith & Farnsworth, 2002), the idea has yet to take hold as a way of thinking about leadership in the academy. Perhaps this is because servant leadership, like transformative leadership, despite its noble ideals, has an implicit sense of noblesse oblige about it.

This same kind of designated-leader thinking plagues other recent writings on shared leadership (e.g., Bradford & Cohen, 1998; Pearce & Conger, 2003)—namely, the assumption that leadership is something for a leader to dole out rather than an opportunity that should be available to all. What's missing in all of these models, whether transformative, servant, or participatory, is the central idea that anyone can lead, right from where they are. Jean Lipman-Blumen (1996) has it exactly right in the preface to her book *The Connective Edge*, in which she asserts:

> Most leadership books have gone off in three directions:
> - The old power-driven, General Patton direction
> - The manipulative, Machiavellian direction
> - More recently, the collaborative, empowering, good-guy direction (p. xi)

She goes on to say:

> Around the globe, two antithetical forces—interdependence and diversity—are generating tensions that will fundamentally change the conditions under which leaders must lead. To succeed in this dramatically altered environment, where inclusion is critical and a connection is inevitable, we need a new kind of leadership. (1996, p. xi)

Just so. Indeed we do. And the need for connectivity is nowhere more pronounced than in the academy. It's high time that academic professionals began taking back the academic leadership they have avoided for so many years. What should this new kind of leadership look like?

A key insight lies in the work of Ronald Heifetz. In 1994 in a book called *Leadership Without Easy Answers*,

Heifetz introduced the notion of what he calls *adaptive work,* or the learning required when neither the problem nor its solution is clearly defined. *Learning* is the key term in adaptive work. Because there are no easy answers in adaptive work—no simple and singular solutions—achieving agreement on a course of action means first that participants must recognize that their existing perspectives won't lead them to a resolution, and second that they must suspend assumptions, entertain fresh questions, and try on the perspectives of others. They must realize that a solution isn't a matter of applying technical solutions more expertly, but rather one of framing problematic situations themselves differently. Thus, if the essence of leadership lies in creating space for important learning to occur, then two implications follow. First, what could be a more obvious setting for leadership as learning than a university? Second, *creating space for learning does not have to reside with people having formal authority.* It can come from anyone with a stake in the organization's future. Academic professionals can lead from where they are without giving up their central roles as academics. Leadership does not have to be hierarchical, formal, or rule bound, but rather lateral, informal, and ad hoc.

Organization of the Book

In the chapters that follow, academic leaders from diverse sectors of the academy tell their stories about leading-in-place. Some are faculty members, and some are administrators; some have sought and embraced their leadership roles, and some have done so reluctantly; some of their stories have a happy ending, and some do not. But each contributes a useful lesson:

- Susanne Morgan, a senior faculty member in a private comprehensive university, introduces a faculty perspective on academic leadership in Chapter 2. She reviews how faculty culture has changed over the past 30-plus years and how challenges and opportunities for faculty leadership in place have—and maybe haven't—changed accordingly.

- In Chapter 3 "Professor X," a faculty member in a large research university, tells a story of "illegitimate" leadership—how a new dean engaged in such egregious practices that the faculty arose from their insularity and became leaders in place. Professor X's story reveals fresh and perhaps surprising insights for faculty leadership under adverse conditions.

- Shelley Chapman and Linda Randall tell a very different story in Chapter 4 about how a new department chair in a research university and a group of mostly part-time faculty came together to undertake a major curricular reform. Chapman and Randall argue that this unlikely alliance was so effective in part because of a deliberate plan by the chair (Randall) to engage in both adaptive leading and transformative learning. They present a model that helps explain how these ideas came together so well. The contrasts between the leadership displayed here and that described by Professor X are stark.

- A similar story is told by Mark Hower and Shana Hormann in Chapter 5. The authors, faculty members (and now administrators) at a small private university, recount another tale of curricular reform led by the faculty. In this case an external review team mandated the change effort, which went beyond curricular reform to a major academic reorganization. Hower and Hormann reflect on factors which helped the faculty move from skepticism to a shared vision.

- In Chapter 6 Victoria Hardy rounds out the stories on faculty-led leadership by describing the paralysis that can occur when someone—in this case an interim faculty leader—has neither formal authority nor sufficient informal authority. Personality conflicts and old politics got in the way of any shared vision, and in the end led to formal mediation.

- In Chapter 7 Carol Reineck, chair of a nursing department at a large health science center, begins a set of chapters on ways those holding positions of formal authority can promote leadership in place by describing a comprehensive self-assessment program in her department. She draws upon her military experience by borrowing the following set of values to undergird the process: loyalty, duty, respect, selfless service, and personal courage.
- Authors of the last three contributed chapters consider how designated leaders can make leadership in place more likely. In Chapter 8 Joseph Barwick, longtime faculty leader and now president of a community college, argues that leadership at any level requires more than simple influence: It requires the ability and desire to encourage others to follow.
- In Chapter 9 Willis Watt reflects on a 30-year career as faculty member, department chair, chief academic officer, and dean, and concludes that three qualities are most important: empowerment, collaboration, and encouragement of risk taking.
- In Chapter 10 Ellen Beatty and Robert Page, vice president for academic affairs and senior faculty member, respectively, at a public comprehensive university, take a different tack. They identify key challenges for higher education leadership and conclude that the times require four leadership dimensions that will be needed to result in the kind of conditions that Watt writes of: consideration, leadership communication, compelling goals/vision, and alignment.

In Chapter 11, I integrate the lessons of the previous nine chapters into an agenda for what higher education must do to create conditions under which leadership in place is the norm rather than the exception.

Between here and there, enjoy the stories.

References

American Library Association. (1998). *Academic librarianship and the Redefining Scholarship Project*. Retrieved August 23, 2006, from: www.ala.org/ala/acrl/acrlpubs/whitepapers/academiclibrarianship.htm

Barbuto, J. E., & Wheeler, D. W. (2005). *Scale development and construct clarification of servant leadership.* Unpublished manuscript.

Bergquist, W. H. (1992). *The four cultures of the academy: Insights and strategies for improving leadership in collegiate organizations.* San Francisco, CA: Jossey-Bass.

Birnbaum, R. (1988). *How colleges work: The cybernetics of academic organization and leadership.* San Francisco, CA: Jossey-Bass.

Block, P. (1995, Fall). Rediscovering service: Weaning higher education from its factory mentality. *Educational Record, 76*(4), 7–13.

Bradford, D. L., & Cohen, A. R. (1998). *Power up: Transforming organizations through shared leadership.* New York, NY: John Wiley & Sons.

Burke, J. C., & Associates. (2005). *Achieving accountability in higher education: Balancing public, academic, and market demands.* San Francisco, CA: Jossey-Bass.

Burns, J. M. (1978). *Leadership.* New York, NY: Harper & Row.

Cook-Sather, A. (2001, Winter). Unrolling roles in techno-pedagogy: Toward new forms of collaboration in traditional college settings. *Innovative Higher Education, 26*(2), 121–139.

Fairweather, J. S. (1996). *Faculty work and public trust: Restoring the value of teaching and public service in American academic life.* Needham Heights, MA: Allyn & Bacon.

Greenleaf, R. K. (1977). *Servant leadership: A journey into the nature of legitimate power and greatness.* Mahwah, NJ: Paulist Press.

Guskin, A. E., & Marcy, M. B. (2003, July/August). Dealing with the future now: Principles for creating a vital campus in a climate of restricted resources. *Change, 35*(4), 10–21.

Heifetz, R. A. (1994). *Leadership without easy answers.* Cambridge, MA: Belknap Press.

Hisle, W. L. (2002). *Top issues facing academic libraries: A report of the Focus on the Future Task Force.* Retrieved August 23, 2006, from the American Library Association web site: www.ala.org/ala/acrl/acrlpubs/crlnews/backissucs 2002/novmonth/topissuesfacing.htm

Keeling, R. P. (Ed.). (2004). *Learning reconsidered: A campus-wide focus on the student experience.* Washington, DC: National Association of Student Personnel Administrators and the American College Personnel Association.

Levine, A. (2000). *Higher education at a crossroads* (Earl V. Pullias Lecture in Higher Education). Los Angeles, CA: University of Southern California, Center for Higher Education Policy Analysis, Rossier School of Education.

Lipman-Blumen, J. (1996). *The connective edge: Leading in an interdependent world.* San Francisco, CA: Jossey-Bass.

Millet, J. (1962). *The academic community: An essay on organization.* New York, NY: McGraw-Hill.

Pearce, C. L., & Conger, J. A. (2003). *Shared leadership: Reframing the hows and whys of leadership.* Thousand Oaks, CA: Sage.

Rosovsky, H. (1990). *The university: An owner's manual.* New York, NY: W. W. Norton & Company.

Smith, R. M., & Farnsworth, K. A. (2002). Servant-leadership in community colleges. In L. C. Spears & M. Lawrence (Eds.), *Focus on leadership: Servant-leadership for the twenty-first century* (pp. 211–222). New York, NY: Wiley.

Wergin, J. F. (2001, Winter). Beyond carrots and sticks: What really motivates faculty. *Liberal Education, 87*(1), 50–53.

Zemsky, R., & Massy, W.F. (1993, May/June). On reversing the ratchet: Restructuring in colleges and universities. *Change, 25*(3), 56–62.

Zemsky, R., & Massy, W. F. (2004). *Thwarted innovation: What happened to e-learning and why.* Philadelphia, PA: The Learning Alliance for Higher Education, University of Pennsylvania.

2

Legacies of Leadership in Place

Susanne Morgan

I began teaching in higher education in 1972, having completed coursework in 1969 and my dissertation in 1971, two weeks after the birth of my first child. I was 27 years old and had never been in a classroom in any leadership role. Since then I've taught full-time in three institutions and part-time in several, with a second child, divorce, health challenges, and other personal tumult along the way.

Now over 60 and nearing 25 years at my current institution, I am in the legacy phase of my career, able to look back with perspective and look forward to retirement and shifting roles. I am thinking a lot about the ways my cohort has changed higher education. I believe that we entered a system that had been relatively stable and we brought about change in the focus and values of the enterprise. We were not entirely successful, of course, and we are leaving an institution that is struggling with challenges we decry.

My leadership during these 30-odd years has paralleled that of many colleagues. We have been leaders in place, moving in and out of formal leadership roles in our institutions. We have also led from the classroom and the research project, introducing ways of thinking and doing that have transformed teaching and scholarship. Many of us have led from outside, particularly in our earlier years. We collaborated with colleagues on and off campus in efforts that formally or informally challenged the existing norms.

In this chapter I tell my own leadership story, softening some of the details for privacy. My focus is primarily on the midsize private comprehensive college where I have worked for most of my years, and on my discipline in the social sciences and my teaching-oriented concentration. Several colleagues' voices are integrated for additional perspective, but I have not carried out a formal interview study.

As you share my reflections, you will see some of the ways my cohort has transformed higher education and the ways we lead within it. You will also glimpse some of the challenges we face as we transfer leadership to the next generation. As you move in and out of your own leadership roles, I hope you find my story helpful.

In 1972 we were part of a vibrant intellectual community. For many of us it seemed to be the natural outcome of the new ways we had been thinking in our undergraduate and graduate programs. Although our own college coursework had probably not challenged political thinking, it had taught us to challenge, to use different lenses, and to see the world in a more complex way than we had known. So with opposition to the war in Vietnam following the civil rights movement and leading to the women's movement, our sense of the established order was disturbed. We had an exciting new way to see and were passionate about sharing it.

We formed small groups with big titles. We were caucuses and associations and societies, and we met and talked about issues of great concern to us. We worked hard, we were smart, and our discussions often became analyses. We planned strategies for improving the lives of our students, our communities, and our colleagues. We wrote essays and position papers and reports and articles. Some of those appeared in campus papers or local newsletters; others were published in journals that were outside our disciplinary organizations.

We almost certainly did not see our actions as leadership; in fact, we saw leadership as part of the problem. Many of our groups were organized to reduce traditional leadership hierarchies and to share leadership behaviors. We were also far younger—and some of us were far more female, more black, or more gay—than the people we considered leaders.

Instead, we saw ourselves as agents of social change, challenging leadership and its priorities. We challenged the leadership of the U.S. to end the war, we challenged the leadership of our institutions to value student learning, and we challenged the leadership of our academic disciplines to expand their scope. Often we were angry about the problems we perceived, and our challenges did not endear us to the leaders.

So we were leading in opposition to, and often outside, our institutions and our disciplinary organizations. We challenged our institutions to let us offer courses from a critical perspective, such as defining social problems as due to inequality rather than to deviant behavior. We wanted to analyze current issues, such as racial segregation, women's reproductive rights, and the war, as central in our courses. We also challenged our institutions to eliminate tenure quotas and to provide fair wages to staff. We tried to press our institutions to implement the affirmative action policies that some had adopted. The problem and the size of our organization seem impossible now, but my first institution, an extremely small "women faculty caucus," successfully challenged the nepotism rule that prevented a married woman from receiving tenure in her husband's department.

In this kind of activity we saw the administration as the enemy, and we were sure they saw us the same way. We thought the campus leaders did not respect the principles that we held most deeply. Apart from any other factors, we dressed far differently from the suits and business dresses of the administration. Like some others, I went so far as to become pregnant, only to be told by my chair there would be no departmental support of any kind and to be asked by my dean, who saw me on campus in my eighth month, why I was still there. No wonder many in my cohort saw, and may still see, institutional leadership as something to avoid!

We also led outside our disciplines. For some young faculty, the research and scholarly or artistic work we did was seen as unprofessional. We may have been pioneers in areas that eventually became central, but at the time we were rebels, and our work was discredited. Research on topics relevant to the researcher was discounted as personal or biased. Few studies in sociology at that time, for instance, dealt with gender as a primary factor or sampled only women. Even fewer attempted an analysis from the point of view of the research subjects. Some scholars persevered in the existing disciplinary conferences and journals, becoming the pioneers of new scholarship. Some founded alternative conferences and periodicals: the Union for Radical Political Economists, the Berkshire Conference on the History of Women, Sociologists for Women in Society, *The Insurgent Sociologist,* and the Health Policy Advisory Center, among many others.

For many young people in the 1970s, it was equally important to extend scholarship out of the academy entirely. We built national journals and newsletters that presented strong research and analysis to the public. At the time, this kind of writing did not count at all in reviews for tenure and promotion. Yet today it is clear that some of that work was very substantial, and the analyses stand the test of time. Most well known in my field is the work of the Boston Women's Health Collective, whose first *Our Bodies, Ourselves* was a newsprint collection of pieces written by a group of women committed to presenting technical information with an analytic perspective to the public. Others included *Science for the People, The Second Wave, Dollars and Sense, HealthRight*, and additional titles that have faded from my memory. Some academically trained people left the institutions entirely and today do very different kinds of work; others have remained marginal to higher education.

As excited as we were about the new perspectives and new analyses we were absorbing, it was natural that we would bring them into our teaching. Teaching has absorbed most of my professional energy and leadership efforts, and my observations reflect that emphasis. We saw our teaching as a major element of our social change work. We wanted to engage students in the critical issues of the day and help them use the tools of our disciplines to do so. Here, too, we made mistakes, but now one can see that we were leading the move to a new kind of college teaching.

My colleagues and I were not alone as we tried to make sense of our jobs: In those days undergraduate institutions were growing very rapidly and new faculty were in great demand. We burst into higher education with the conviction that we would make a difference. Many of us had been deeply influenced by the civil rights movement of our adolescence and college years and yearned to embody the moral principles of our heroes. On our campuses the U.S. presence in Vietnam was a contentious issue, and many of us were deeply ambivalent about our roles as teachers and scholars. Few of our colleagues had served in Vietnam, because of student deferments, and more of our students were engaged in activism. We knew that many of our older colleagues thought activism was unprofessional for faculty, but to us it seemed natural to use our intellectual training to understand the events around us.

The women's movement was in its second wave. Most of us never had female professors as undergraduate or graduate students. Few of us who were women had female mentors, and the existing models of professional careers did not include family obligations: Our models usually had wives. It was confusing even to understand our disciplines in light of the new feminism. I still recall feeling a deep thrill when I heard a conference paper that used "she" instead of the generic "he" and my shame when a colleague pointed out the unfortunate title of the text I used: *Sociology: Man in Society* (Scott Foresman, 1971). I had gone through a Ph.D. in sociology, somehow believing that everything I learned did not really apply to me.

We were trying to figure out who we were and what our job was, and it was even harder to understand who the students were. Many were dramatically unlike the students we had been just ten years earlier. More than half the students were older than I was, and I was regularly assumed to be a student or a secretary. They were also far worldlier than we were, having lived harder lives and made tougher choices than we had. Particularly at the public urban university where I first taught, students were activists about their education as well as about national politics. Many of them developed incisive critiques of the university, many demanded accountability, and they did not always treat us with the deference we anticipated. Our students used the analytic tools of our disciplines in innovative ways, but often they used a writing style and tone that did not meet our academic expectations. So should we grade the ideas or the writing? How should we separate the politics from the written work? How should we engage classroom discussion yet maintain order? How should we treat women and minority students, and how, if we were women or minority faculty, should we present ourselves?

We had few models for teaching strategies other than lecture. Terms like *pedagogy, strategies,* and *objectives* were not in our vocabularies; they applied to K–12 teaching, and we definitely felt we were above that. Most of our departments did not require student evaluations in the sense of systematic responses from students. Our job was presenting our discipline to students; theirs was to understand and appreciate its intrinsic relevance and value.

We tried. We tried to include contemporary examples in our lectures. We tried to open our classrooms to discussion beyond our lecture. We tried to develop reading and writing assignments that made connections between our analyses and their world. We tried to think about the students as active participants. We tried to grade their work less punitively than our older colleagues appeared to.

We stumbled, of course. We couldn't always keep discussions from becoming arguments. We made some lame assignments that prompted rhetorical rather than analytic responses. We imagined that we were far more egalitarian than we in fact were, and we often didn't recognize the real power differences between us and our students.

But in the end we have indeed been leaders, and our generation has indeed transformed college teaching. We were part of the shift that moved students into the picture of academic work and even closer to the center. We were leaders in our departments as we tried to establish the systematic use of student evaluations in assessment of teaching. Some of us even campaigned for student participation in departmental discussions of curriculum and even of personnel issues.

We led by being what is now called scholarly teachers: We read *Radical Teacher* and the fledgling periodicals on teaching in our disciplines and in higher education. Some of us led by organizing colleagues and persisting until our institutions formed and supported centers for teaching.

Our cohort also nurtured the beginnings of the scholarship of teaching and learning. The early members of the Professional and Organizational Development Network for Higher Education (POD Network), for example, were passionate about improving teaching, evaluating the success of trials, and sharing the results with the wider public. They did not see themselves as national leaders, although many have become exactly that. They saw themselves as reducing their individual isolation and improving their work, and in so doing they brought about a new scholarship.

The same is true with disciplinary scholarship. After bitterly decrying the values and orientation of our disciplines, we have seen them incorporate much of what we stood for. We have taken our turns in leadership positions in disciplinary organizations. Many of us are highly distinguished scholars largely on our own terms: Our disciplines have shifted to embrace many of our positions. Others have remained disaffected and have never reintegrated into the disciplinary scholarship that excited us so much in our youth.

As a cohort, then, we began leading from outside, and often against, our institutions. We didn't trust our institutions, because they really did not value the kinds of work we valued: teaching, flatter hierarchy, more participation. Today we can see that in many ways we have succeeded. Institutions have changed dramatically since 1972, and many of our core values are institutionalized. In fact, many of us are now the official academic leaders. We are the ones who have repeatedly been leaders in place, moving into official leadership roles and back into the faculty. Many of us are seen as valued institutional citizens, and some have become full-time administrators.

It could appear that my effort is to glorify my generation or to claim that we have created an ideal higher education system. Of course, that is not my intent, and there is a great deal that is very wrong in higher education. My goal is to help younger generations understand us better and to help my cohort realize some of the challenges that remain.

There were many challenges of leading in place in my cohort. Our younger colleagues who see us as the senior statesmen and women may not realize that at first we had to lead against the administration. If we didn't, we were thought to be colluding in oppression and were not trusted by our own peers. This has led, for some of us, to deep confusion about the roles of leaders and the power and authority that leaders may or may not have.

Sometimes it has been hard to take ourselves seriously as leaders and to realize that people look up to us. Even if we understood that we could have brought about the changes we valued by holding official leadership positions, many of us have resisted those positions. It has often been difficult to use the authority we do have, because we have not fully integrated our early beliefs with the demands of formal leadership roles. Some of us have not been as effective leaders as we might have been and have made strategic errors in our leadership.

When I was tenured, I became chairperson of my department in the mid 1980s, and it was tough. Most of my colleagues were the same age; we had belonged to many leaderless groups in our formative years, and we shared the assumption that power was bad and the chair should only do the necessary functions. Yet we were all teachers and had power in that realm: What we told students to do in the classroom was what happened. As chairperson I couldn't just plan a syllabus and tell colleagues what to do as if they were students, but we were not a leaderless group with a common mission that I could facilitate. I didn't know how to be a leader from within a group when that group was embedded in a complex structure with specific responsibilities for the chair.

In addition to cohort, and gender of course, there are other elements that can contribute to challenges in leadership. For me personally, coming from a very small rural Midwestern area also affected my leadership. I assumed that everyone knew who I was and that I didn't have to do anything particular to have an identity. In my community in the 1950s, one knew people by their identity and relationships, not primarily by their roles. In a city one is known initially in terms of a role. So it was harder for me personally to understand the role expectations of a professor. Combining that with a changing set of role expectations in the 1970s, leadership became even more confusing. Like others, I had the confidence, perhaps false, that one's leadership is appreciated as part of one's identity. I probably did not recognize how very challenging some of my community-building activities were.

This particular experience may also be true for faculty who are from working-class backgrounds or members of ethnic groups. Others have observed that as people enter the white middle class, the unwritten rules are very real but hard to understand. In academia, I believe that people from small towns have somewhat similar experiences. With the sense of not knowing the rules comes a kind of blundering into leadership without internal guidelines about the character of different leadership roles. So we may not be very strategic about leadership in the academy.

Those personal characteristics may be part of the reason that much of my leadership has been largely outside the more formal institutional structure. I worked with student affairs professionals to organize important student groups and campaigns. Although the work has indeed changed the institution, I did not see it as leadership. Leadership had committee names or titles. For me, my activities provided a direction for my passion and a way to feel less isolated and more connected in the institution.

On every campus there are many faculty members of my cohort who still see the academic world as "us" versus "them"—who reflexively resist the administration on nearly every issue. I think this is understandable; many of us have very deep scars. Many of us have not moved from our first jobs, because colleges were growing so fast when we were starting out. If someone has worked an entire career in the same institution, it can be hard to let go of the past.

I think many of us find it hard to let go, either of our aloof and superior position outside or of our bloody struggles within. It can be hard to accept new faculty members who don't see things as we do. They don't see the need to be so separate and don't see why we are sometimes so negative about our institutions or so divorced from our disciplines.

But of course our new faculty members do not see the world as we do. They have known nothing except the higher education that we created. We did move student learning into the center, undergraduate teaching into valued jobs, and higher education into the communities. And now we hire faculty whom we taught as undergraduates, sometimes literally. We are hiring faculty who want to teach undergraduates, who understand the richness and variety of fluid disciplines, and who assume that teaching, scholarship, and service can be authentic parts of a satisfying life.

In my excellent comprehensive college peopled by many age peers, I see problems with our legacy. We were passionate 30 years ago and remain dedicated to our work, but we've helped to create some difficult situations. The following are some imaginary departments. Readers are invited to think about the ways leaders in place could move these departments forward.

- The Department of Protection Studies has senior faculty who are very aware of the differences in power and security between us and the newer faculty. And we are so concerned to protect those newer faculty members that we don't treat them as authentic colleagues. We project onto them our anxiety about the current standards for tenure and may guide them to such narrow definitions of excellence that we don't let them develop their own professional identities.

Leaders need to know the facts and not rely on the gossip about retention decisions. From outside the department, we need to convince our colleagues that interdisciplinary teaching, pedagogical variety, or engagement in campus-wide initiatives is not so dangerous. To the contrary, engaging in those activities may be central to the mission and strategic plan of the institution. Visible support from institutional leaders at the same or higher positions as the senior faculty can help the newer faculty contextualize their work and the senior faculty appreciate it. If the institution is changing to include a wider definition of our work, then leaders in place must not subvert that transition by an inconsistent stance on criteria.

- The Department of Second-Class Studies was built by faculty members who were convinced that we really belonged at a more prestigious institution and have carried some level of resentment for 30 years. Newer faculty see this in our tendency to disparage students and not really notice how much stronger the students have become. We are often seen as extremely harsh critics of newer faculty members, who sometimes wonder if we are repeating what was done to us in the old days.

This department calls for strong leadership inside and outside to support our excellent new faculty members. Although some in higher education see newer faculty members as lacking the energy for leadership, the picture on campuses like mine may be different. People make deliberate choices to work at our institutions, and teaching-oriented positions are much more highly valued than they were when we began our careers. The institution must devise strategies to nurture the leadership within the newer cohort and create a culture of engagement.

- The Department of Fiefdom Studies had strong individual faculty members with clear curricular and research agendas. It was natural 30 years ago to organize based on the models around us in graduate schools. Now the newer faculty members are bewildered by the competitiveness and possessiveness of the senior faculty. They see the departmental tasks and resources as something to be shared and see us as obstructing their attempts to simply get on with the business at hand.

Similar to the Department of Second-Class Studies, this department calls for leaders in place who move forward despite the reluctance of senior members. Leaders from the newer cohort could quietly move around the fiefdoms, working collaboratively to set the tone and organizational structure for the future. Institutional leaders could establish the model of a legacy project, funding, or other incentives to support the feudal lords to intentionally plan the inheritance of the fiefdoms.

- The Department of Us-and-Them Studies is populated by proud progressives, and we have hired newer faculty members who also have a critical perspective. The newer faculty members, however, do not seem to challenge the administration enough. They think, probably correctly, that the administration appreciates their work, but we remain skeptical and suspect that the newer faculty members are being used for the (perhaps evil) purposes of the administration.

For a variety of reasons, our newer faculty members do not show the fire for reform that characterized my generation. Reform remains necessary, although its focus will be different, and as senior leaders we need to be vigilant that the institution does not punish innovation or reform. The tricky part will be that the direction of reform may seem to us to be either not radical enough or radical in the wrong way. In other situations, we may see the newer faculty's challenges as trivial and contradictory to the well-being of the institution. We need to protect the institutional mechanisms for analysis and change that we struggled to implement. We also need to prod the newer faculty members to go beyond our vision in how they imagine the institutions they inherit.

- The Department of Collegiality Studies was characterized for decades by bitter divisions among the long-term faculty members. Now that several have retired, we fervently want peace and unanimity. So we seem to attack newer faculty who question or challenge us. To the newer faculty members, it seems that we are recreating divisions in the name of collegiality. They are finding their voice, and it appears that we are trying to silence them.

Institutional leaders must maintain structures through which faculty members can make a difference, even if the difference is not what the senior faculty members might suggest. The newer cohort of faculty is more diverse than we were, although we differed dramatically from our predecessors. Senior colleagues can connect with their peers to discuss ways to help the newer faculty find their own voice across campus.

- The Department of Flexibility Studies built a successful program that employed many faculty members on part-time and short-term contracts. Those in my cohort don't understand the objections to these flexible jobs, even though they may have worked for us decades ago. Newer faculty members see them as ways that permanently marginal careers are created and maintained.

Leaders from my generation take for granted that faculty members are invested in their institutions. We were deeply committed, even if committed to battle. We need now to use our institutional influence to maintain a core faculty of full-time professors to whom the institution is committed. Otherwise, who will do the major work of the institution, in curriculum, in reviewing faculty, and in the other areas where seeing the big picture is crucial?

- The Department of Baby-Card Studies includes a set of bewildered young faculty members who don't understand why their activist senior colleagues seem to obstruct their efforts to create a balanced life. We note that we had to deal with heavy work and young children, and we say they should not "play the baby card." But we forget that the purpose of our struggles was to improve the lives of the next generation, and we forget that these young faculty members are figuratively our children, whom we taught to value a balanced life.

Senior leaders need to figure out how to support institutional engagement among newer faculty members even while family is a priority. Some seem to say, "What I do doesn't matter; so I just do my job." This can represent two unanticipated effects of our leadership. We have brought the person into the workplace, so it is natural that faculty would want a full and balanced life. But we have also permitted institutions to move to structural arrangements that do not support faculty as full people, so it is natural that they would see their loyalties as not primarily to the institution. The newer faculty members have answers to these challenges; we need to hear them and use our influence to implement them.

The new generations of leaders in place will not have the same challenges that we faced, and they probably don't understand them. They will have their own challenges, however, and the institutions will grow from vibrant leaders in place. What advice can those of us in the legacy phase offer our newer colleagues?

Be gentle with us. We probably don't remember the confusion and bewilderment we felt when we were in your stage of leadership, so we probably seem very sure of ourselves. Stay patient with our pronouncements, even if you disagree, and understand that we, like you, have always done our very best.

Name our leadership. We may be authentically ignorant of our own institutional importance, and we may be intimidated by your accomplishments. Please don't fawn over us, but do notice!

Build relationships with us. We are not as unlike you as we seem, or we may be far more unlike you than it appears. Our stories are stories of an era that is passing, and we will all be glad if we pass our inheritance to people we know.

We are proud of what our leadership has accomplished. We are also deeply concerned about our institutions, and we believe that the leaders in place will continue to work for the best of our values and goals. I add my voice to the others in this volume and remind us all to nurture our colleagues as they move in and out of leadership roles.

Acknowledgments

Thanks to Jon Wergin for ideas and editing.

3

(Leading?) From the Core

"Professor X"

Editor's note: In order to protect the people and institution discussed in this chapter, the author chose to use a pseudonym so as not to reveal identity or professional affiliation.

The title of this chapter has several meanings. One, when I started as a tenure-track faculty member 12 years ago, my School of Education was organized into "cores" rather than departments—small units such as counseling or educational leadership that were, in turn, part of larger units, namely divisions. How is this relevant to the story I'm about to tell? Well, I personally don't think that organizational structures per se matter terribly much in my life as a faculty member, but it was the *transition* from cores to departments and the very way in which this transition was initiated and implemented that are illustrative of much of what seems to ail the academy today. In Chapter 1 Jon Wergin described this as hijacking the term *transformative leadership* in order to transform in a unilateral fashion. On one level, then, my story is about how *not* to lead, and my school's transformation from cores to departments may well serve as illustration.

Second, I argue that the core of why academics became academics in the first place—what Jon referred to as our academic calling—might well be the nexus of much needed change in the academy. Before I tell the story about cores in my school and what I consider to be the core of change, however, I begin with some introductory comments about the very concept of leadership and the business of writing a "persofessional tale" (a tale that is rather personal in a professional sense), like the one I offer here.

Background

I was born and raised in Germany and educated primarily in Germany, with international study experiences in the U.S. and Canada. I was in my late twenties when I came to the U.S. to pursue my doctorate and stay. This is important to consider, because when I first heard conversations involving leadership, my reaction was rather visceral. *Leader* means *führer* in German, not a term with which I associate anything positive.

It was puzzling to me how intellectuals in the very country that prides itself on being the "number-one democracy in the world" can spend so much energy on aspiring to prepare for and become successful leaders, however defined. Leaders are only able to be leaders if there are followers, and preparing a society in which there are both leaders and followers strikes me as an inherently undemocratic notion. How would I feel if the teacher of my eight-year-old son announced one day that he is preparing the child to become a "successful follower?" How would any parent feel? It took me a long time to understand (and, quite honestly, I am to this day not certain that I really do) that when people talk about leaders they simply mean good, strong people who tend to work for something beyond their self-interest (clearly a connotation of the term *servant-leadership*). Nevertheless, a certain degree of uneasiness vis-à-vis the term *leadership* remains to the point where I could not even bring myself to omit the parentheses in the title of this chapter.

Before I begin the tale I want to emphasize that I am deeply loyal to my institution, both to the School of Education and the university at large, because they have given me an intellectual home where I am able to do the work I love to do. It is a good place, warts and all, and so I am still in my "first job" with no intention to go anywhere else. Part of this story is not pretty, however, and discloses some rather dirty laundry. I appeal to the reader to treat it as you would treat dirty laundry in a family: a simple fact of life, not an indication of dysfunctionality.

The End of an Era and the Ascent of an "Illegitimate Leader"

For 16 years my school was led by a dean who had come from the ranks of the faculty and, in his kind and unassuming way, had enjoyed the faculty's trust. He was not one to make a big splash and in that way was perhaps not the most effective representative of the school in terms of bringing in and securing funds, for example. He was not a player in a political sense, but he was seen as one of us, a straight shooter whom we trusted, and someone who was leading the school not because he had some bloated idea of what an administrator is but very simply because someone had to do it. He was an example of what some of us believe to be the best kind of administrator: one who never wanted the job in the first place. The dean saw himself as primarily serving the faculty whose role, in turn, was to educate the students and engage in scholarship and service. That, after all, is what the university is all about in a nutshell. The dean sought to support us to the best of his abilities so that we were able to do our work. He had one assistant dean for student affairs and was supported by three very capable division heads and a reasonable number of staff persons serving various functions we never much cared to understand in any depth.

The dean retired. Actually, one should not say "retired" because it has become customary for our administrators and some faculty to retire and then come back. They return in some rather obscure administrative function or as adjunct faculty member, and the primary reason for their return seems to be the individual maximization of retirement benefits. These reappearing acts are sometimes welcomed by the faculty; perhaps it depends on who does the reappearing and what the person does once he or she is back. If their reappearance is not perceived as useful or necessary, we tend to see it as a drain on funds that should more productively be spent on new full-time faculty members. Be that as it may, what I just described is but one example of hiring practices in sync with the national trend at colleges and universities to replace full-time, tenure-track work with part-time, non-tenure-track appointments. Such practices borrowed from the corporate world, after all, are much more conducive to the quick hiring and firing of an increasingly docile labor force. One could tell many stories about the leadership challenges created when a university community stands by and does virtually nothing about the growing exploitation of part-time faculty, particularly adjunct faculty—but I digress.

The old dean retired or at least left his post as dean and the school faced a power vacuum. Initially, an interim dean rose from the ranks of the faculty and served for a year, eventually exhausted primarily by an unprecedented budget crisis. After that instead of following the conventional process and conducting a thorough search for the most qualified person to fill the job, our university administration planted a person in the position. This new dean had never enjoyed the status of a legitimate faculty member: He had never followed the hiring practices, such as committee interviews, quite commonplace in an institution that is essentially faculty governed. No, this dean came to the school after serving many years in leadership positions in the public school systems. The faculty was never sure how he had come to join our ranks and suspected it had been done for his political clout. He was perceived to be a skillful political player who knew the relevant politicians in the state and was in that sense possibly an asset for the school. This is the way he became a faculty member, and this is the way some years later he became our dean. The faculty, by and large, was aghast.

One important lesson here to be learned for leadership studies is that the *process* of how someone rises to a leadership position is of utmost importance. I am not a student of leadership studies and, as pointed out earlier, have in the past done my best to avoid the issue altogether. I am assuming that there is literature available documenting the point just made. Be that as it may, this story would certainly be an illustration. I am not sure that the new dean ever had a chance to earn the respect and acceptance of his faculty given the way he was planted. He had no legitimacy in our eyes. An exceptional personality, however, might have been able to overcome such obstacles. As one faculty member aptly put it: "People can learn. They have ways to adapt to different cultures. He could have done so as well." Strong leaders are adaptive, willing to change and see the world through new perspectives and on the basis of new paradigms. They try to understand the peculiarities of the context in which they find themselves, take nothing for granted, and adapt their ways as necessary.

In our case a successful dean needed to be someone who understood faculty culture and faculty thinking, not that those are monolithic or easy to peck, to be sure. But one very important tenet of faculty culture, I think, is that regardless of where a leader comes from or how he or she assumes a certain position, faculty need to get the sense, based on evidence and behavior and not mere proclamations, that things are real, that promises are not empty, and that processes are not merely window dressing. This was perhaps the single biggest mistake the new dean made: Once he was told (and we literally had to tell him) that the faculty valued shared governance and wished to be involved in decision-making processes, he had all of us go through the motions of pseudodemocratic processes while, in the end, making decisions based solely on his prerogatives.

The new dean was a former public school superintendent who thought of a school of education in the same way he thought of a school system. While I am not convinced that the bureaucracy that undergirds our public school system is the "one best system" (Tyack, 1974), I do know that even if it worked for K–12, it does not work as a model for a university entity, any more than the corporate model works. Universities are neither school systems nor businesses. They differ significantly in terms of their history, organizational structure, and culture. Our dean did not understand this. Without discussion he began to expand the traditional triangle of faculty responsibilities—scholarship, teaching, and service—by adding the concept of "entrepreneurship." The faculty objected, explaining that there are centuries of higher education history involved in the traditional triad and that there are good reasons why it has withstood the test of time.

Examples of the new dean's unsuccessful leadership style abound, but for the purpose of this chapter a select few will suffice.

Corrupting the Structure

Moves Without Meaning

One of the first moves the new dean initiated was the reorganization of the school around departments rather than cores. His rationale was that such a move would save money, because we would no longer need division heads. It should be noted that the division heads in our school were trusted long-term and full-time administrators whom the faculty cherished as staunch advocates, competent mentors, and workhorses, taking care of all the big and little things that made the place work. Getting rid of them cut deeply into the social and professional fabrics of our lives. Furthermore, the math simply did not work here, because while the division head positions were abandoned, a total of eight departments were formed, all of which required the hiring of department chairs—faculty who assumed department chair functions for extra pay. Additionally, the new dean hired two assistant/associate deans and what seemed like an army of administrative staff to support him. What his true motives for the reorganization were, nobody knows to this day. He had promised that we would revisit the reorganization of the school after a while but, when reminded to do so after one year, refused to live up to that promise in any meaningful way. The faculty was left with a deepening sense of distrust.

Corrupting the Decision-Making Process

A second example of unsuccessful leadership concerned the new dean's misuse of established processes. He formed faculty advisory committees, for example, on which faculty were asked to serve, but we soon understood that the sole purpose of these committees was to legitimize the decisions the dean wanted to make. He simply needed to be able to say "*we* decided" rather than "*I* decided." Pretty soon, a vicious cycle had been generated. When the dean made unilateral decisions, the faculty felt left out; when he solicited input, we did not trust the process.

Interfering With Faculty Prerogatives

One tenet of higher education that nearly everyone understands is that curricular decisions fall squarely into the realm of the faculty. The dean was unaware of this and made promises to large numbers of school administrators in several school districts to provide them with accelerated Ph.D. programs, or quick-and-dirty degrees, without consulting with the faculty or considering whether we had enough faculty to provide such programs. When the faculty balked, the dean found himself in a self-generated dilemma and in peril of publicly losing face, because he had made deals he could not honor. We bailed him out and agreed to teach the students he recruited and guide them through the dissertation process under the condition that he refrain from such practices. Nevertheless, the dilemma of trying to serve doctoral students without the resources to do so would be with us for years to come.

Leadership in Place: How to Be Faculty Leaders Under Adverse Conditions

It seems to me that many of the qualities typically associated with strong and successful leaders, such as initiative, creativity, and the ability to see and act upon big-picture ideas, are relatively easy to develop and use in a morally good environment. Put simply, it is often quite easy to be good in a good place. It is no coincidence that we talk about circumstances that bring out the best in people: These circumstances are typically supportive, positive, nurturing, and encouraging. Writing about K–12 schooling, educational philosopher Nel Noddings (2002) reminds us that we should "concentrate on establishing the conditions most likely to support moral life. We want schools to be places where it is both possible and attractive to be good" (p. 9). Now consider the opposite. George Orwell (1946/1981) wrote about his bad school memories using the following words: "I was in a world where it was not *possible* for me to be good . . . Life was more terrible, and I was more wicked, than I had imagined" (Orwell, 1946/1981, p. 5). In general, oppressive or negative conditions tend to discourage good behavior. While extreme

adversity in the form of disasters, emergencies, and crises might bring out heroic behavior in some people, these
are only temporary responses. Far more detrimental for
the flourishing of leadership is the slowly corrosive and
mundane—a deceptive environment in which people are
led to believe that they matter, only to find that they have
just been used in yet another pseudoprocess. Initiative
dies a slow and painful death when subjected to systemic
hoop jumping and meaningless bureaucratic exercises.

That said, I should point out that I am not suggest-
ing (although it may by now seem like it) that an entire
faculty's downfall could hinge upon one person's poor
leadership. That could hardly be true. The challenge we
faced was the result of several factors, including a severe
budget crunch, the drastic decimation of the faculty due
to retirements and inability to replace those retirees, in
addition to poor school leadership. So, what did we do?

Leadership From the Core

Emergence of Various Leaders at Different Levels

Several cells of resistance emerged within the school,
and people within these cells developed leadership qualities in different ways. What did *not* happen was the Hol-
lywoodesque emergence of one person, a John Wayne
of the faculty, who stepped up to challenge the dean on
behalf of the rest of the faculty. Instead, different people assumed different kinds of roles, given their backgrounds and positions, in order to lead in place and, in
subtle or not so subtle ways, effect change for the better. The former division heads and even the former dean,
given their wealth of experience and great institutional
memory, quietly made suggestions from the sidelines as
to how to use the policies and procedures of the institution to assert faculty rights. The president of the faculty organization presided over meetings that reached
record levels of attendance and served as a lifeline of

communication and strategic planning. The department chairs struggled to fulfill their new roles, trying to bridge administrative duties and faculty roles.

Constant Communication

One of the indications of a strong leadership culture, it seems to me, is a healthy flow of communication, through official and unofficial channels, or "hallway conversations." We heavily relied on both of those while trying to reclaim our school. The official communication needed to be handled with care. We had to make sure we followed established processes and communicated our positions through appropriate channels. This wasn't because we were hoping to get through to the dean: We had little evidence of effective communication with him, and I cannot think of one single example where the faculty actually felt heard on an issue. Nevertheless, we needed to exhaust proper communication channels even if the intention was no longer to get the dean to listen. We followed protocol in order to make it legitimate and safe for us to talk among ourselves and to get all parts of the faculty to listen and to support reform ideas. It would have been too scary to be openly subversive; education faculty generally are not known for their radicalism, and we needed to follow proper procedure and play by the book to avoid antagonizing faculty who did not view themselves as change agents but simply as teachers and scholars trying to do their work.

Collectivism and Individualism

One of the dynamics unfolding in our school was a back-and-forth movement of faculty between political activism directed at changing the school and retreat to our individual niches. Leading from the core for me meant that I needed to find a balance among my concerns for the institution, being politically active, and making sure I refueled to maintain the drive and energy to keep going. That drive, interestingly enough, came directly from my passion for what I do. In other words, what is often touted as being in opposition to faculty collaboration—namely faculty individualism—grounded me during turbulent times. I believe this to be true for my colleagues as well. We may not share exactly the same degree of passion for one particular subject, but we do mostly share an intense interest in our respective specializations. As anthropologist Karen B. Strier (2005) stated: "My commitment and passion for my science is a part of me. It's part of who I am" (p. A10).

It is that passion for very specialized knowledge and that interest in very specific questions that makes us academics pursue Ph.D.s in our areas of interest in the first place. It is this passion that propels us to continue to study and learn and write and research and teach about them, often through challenging times of graduate student poverty or other adverse conditions. It is the passion for certain intellectual questions that is at the core of academia. And to this core, or academic calling, I returned repeatedly during the trying times at our school in order to refuel and find the strength to continue to lead in place.

To be sure, exceptions exist. Some academics burn out or become so cynical that it seems as if not much passion is left of any kind and certainly not passion for their field. As a whole, however, I would contend that my colleagues feel deeply connected to what they do on an emotional and an intellectual level. Intellectual work in our field is our essence; it is the reason we entered academia and stayed. It is from that core that the determination to improve one's department, school, or college stems.

Conclusion

Neither my colleagues nor I ever thought much about the concept of leadership, and none of us are scholars in that area. We harbor no aspirations to become leaders in academe other than indirectly through such things as teaching innovations, expansion of the existing knowledge base in our fields and other scholarly insights, and service work to our professional communities and the public. We became leaders in place because we felt that we had no other choice. It became clear to us that we needed to become active and find ways to deal with political structures that undermined the sense of who we were as scholars, as teachers, and as academicians. Our actions did not result from theory or dogma; they resulted from repeated insults on something central to the professoriate, namely shared university governance. Knowing that at times processes are not merely formalities but safeguards of the greater good, we needed to find ways to deal with an illegitimate leader who had risen to power through the back door. A proper search process for a dean's position is one such way.

Furthermore, it was necessary to find ways to bring about change and fight for the preservation of values and ideas we considered to be at the heart of shared governance—a concept we don't cling to dogmatically but wish to preserve because it is the only way to enable us to do what we do well. We actually do know best how to provide quality instruction and guidance to doctoral students, and this should not be changed because someone has an idea he or she finds financially attractive or politically opportune. Research and scholarship are important aspects of our identity and work, and we cannot allow that to be ignored just because our dean has political clout but no background in or understanding of what it means to be an academician. My colleagues and I, in short, had no need for pseudoprocesses or going through the motions in order to preserve the image of joint decision-making. Instead, we insisted on honest approaches and transparency of leadership. It was, however, of utmost importance to us that faculty culture be respected rather than ignored or confused with the cultures of corporations or public school systems.

Institutions of higher education have a long and rich history, and although my colleagues and I are by no means convinced that all traditions are worth preserving, we do agree that they are at least worth knowing.

So, why were we able to develop leadership qualities in what had deteriorated to a rather bad environment, given that leadership qualities typically flourish in good place? My sense is that it happened because we once had a well functioning organization, and at least tacitly understood our rights and the nature of the framework within which we wanted to operate. To put it differently, we had for a long time worked in a good environment and thus remembered more or less instinctively what that looked like.

Be that as it may, our leadership in place entailed the emergence of various leaders in different capacities, sometimes displaying wisdom, common sense, basic civility, courage, or, if all else failed, simply a good sense of humor. Yet there were no heroes; people just attempted to quietly change the system for the better. We used different means of communication and tried to use proper channels whenever possible. While collectivism was necessary and community cherished, a major source of energy resided in our individual passions for our respective fields of work. In fact, it is no exaggeration to say that our rootedness in our disciplines and our strong wish to preserve our work were the driving forces that provided the motivation to strive for an environment conducive to working successfully as the type of academicians we want to be.

Epilogue

What happened to the "illegitimate dean" and these faculty members who became leaders in place? We'll never know for sure exactly what transpired, but the dean eventually stepped down and was replaced by an interim dean. This person (the former dean of faculty affairs) was intimately familiar with the trials and tribulations of the faculty in preceding years. More importantly, however, she had learned to read and understand faculty culture and was not about to play games. The spirit changed instantly. We concluded just weeks into her term as interim dean that although the challenges and difficult issues we had been grappling with had not gone away, our trust in the leadership had been restored. We were finally able to go back to our original missions of being successful faculty, whether leaders or not.

References

Noddings, N. (2002). *Educating moral people: A caring alternative to character education.* New York, NY: Teachers College Press.

Orwell, G. (1981). *A collection of essays.* San Diego, CA: Harcourt Brace. (Original work published 1946)

Strier, K. B. (2005, June 10). My commitment and passion for science is a part of me [Interview]. *The Chronicle of Higher Education, 51*(40), A10.

Tyack, D. B. (1974). *The one best system: A history of American urban education.* Cambridge, MA: Harvard University Press.

4

Adaptive Leadership and Transformative Learning: A Case Study of Leading by Part-Time Faculty

Shelley A. Chapman, Linda M. Randall

I magine joining a new department as its chairperson and inheriting a master's degree program with complex problems: The department's multiple courses have proliferated, nearly all of the faculty are part-time, and enrollment is declining. What would you do? There are no easy solutions or quick fixes to problems such as these, and there are no department chairperson super-heroes who can fly in and save the day. These kinds of problems are common across disciplines, but in this case, the solution to this problem was not common. This chapter is the story of how the part-time faculty not only led the way to create a new master's degree program, but also began the hard work of changing the culture. It is a story of giving voice to typically margin-alized faculty. The case reveals a department chairper-son's trust in the part-time faculty and in the processes of adaptive leading and transformative learning. The cultural transformation that took place, using part-time faculty as part of the process of curriculum design and development, was informed by the adaptive leadership model, based on the work of Ronald Heifetz (1994) and the transformative learning model as developed by Jack Mezirow (1991).

Adaptive Leadership Model

Heifetz (1994) describes adaptive leadership as an approach through which leaders differentiate between two kinds of problem solving: technical and adaptive. Technical problems are not unimportant, and they are not always easy; however, their solutions come from the repertoire of responses we have created through our experiences in the past. For instance, if our car breaks down, we take it to a mechanic for repair. In the classroom, a technical problem might be not having a roster before our class begins. Faculty know that to rectify a problem like this: One would go to a certain 'office or person and request a new roster. Solutions to technical problems are already known.

When solutions to problems are not easily known, and when the problem itself is not easily understood, Heifetz (1994) says we need to seek adaptive solutions. Business and public life offer many examples of adaptive challenges, such as globalization, rapidly changing markets, national debt, failing schools, crime, and racial prejudice (Heifetz & Laurie, 1999). They are adaptive challenges because an authoritative response would not be enough. For these problems, there are no known solutions. In the case discussed in this chapter, the new department chairperson faced a complex set of problems related to the master's degree program, including a decrease in enrollment, an increase in the number of courses offered, and few full-time faculty.

An adaptive leader will first identify the problem as one that requires an adaptive solution and then give the work back to the people involved, because the solution will require learning on their part. Learning for adaptive challenges requires people to change their values, beliefs, attitudes, and habits of behavior. The problem lies in the fact that the people must change, and, therefore, the locus of responsibility for problem solving must shift from those in authority to the stakeholders themselves. This kind of undertaking is difficult, because people generally want solutions without the hard work of relinquishing deeply held beliefs, changing old attitudes, adjusting work habits, and, in essence, learning new ways of being.

Transformative Learning Model

Although there are no easy answers for an adaptive leader, it is clear that learning must take place. Mezirow (1996) differentiates between instrumental learning, learning to control or manipulate the environment or other people, and communicative learning—seeking the meaning and significance of their assumptions, beliefs, and values. Mezirow (1978) says that adults are trapped by their histories and in need of the ability to reflect upon assumptions that are the products of years of socialization and experience. An adult learner's most important responsibility is perhaps the questioning of assumptions. This is adult learning—when the learners can examine previously held presuppositions, frames of reference that lie below the surface of their awareness, and critique those positions in ways that allow for change and growth. When this happens, their "taken-for-granted frames of reference become more inclusive, discriminating, open, emotionally capable of change, and reflective so that they may generate beliefs and opinions that will prove more true or justified to guide action" (Mezirow, 2000, pp. 7–8). Often, transformative learning is a major structural shift in consciousness as a result of reflecting critically on the frames of reference one holds. This type of learning is not simply a heightened sense of new understandings. It involves shifting paradigms or worldviews. It is this kind of learning in which the part-time faculty needed to engage in order to seek adaptive solutions to their complex problem.

Case: Part-Time Faculty Rebuilding a Graduate Program

The academic department at the university was of concern to the school's administration as admissions and enrollments for the master's program directed through this department had been in a constant decline for six to seven years. During its heyday, the program was nationally ranked in the top 15 in its field and enrolled about 140 students per year. At the time roughly 105–110 students enrolled each year, and the decline was not abating. The administration decided that a new chairperson was needed to overhaul the department and program.

The administration decided that it would be more effective to recruit a new chairperson from outside the university. The new chairperson was hired and was charged by the dean to determine whether to continue the program and, if so, in what manner. The department was atypical of most academic units, because it had about 60 adjunct faculty and five full-time faculty (including the chairperson). The department's adjunct faculty taught nearly 70% of the classes for the master's program.

The immediate challenge the new chairperson noted was the proliferation of courses. Depending on the faculty—both full-time and adjunct—the course content and rigor varied. Because of declining enrollments and increasing stop-outs (i.e., students not taking any courses for at least three continuous semesters), many classes would cancel, which angered and discouraged both students and adjuncts.

The new chairperson realized that adjuncts were critical to the success of the program, yet many adjuncts had become disheartened about teaching in the program. As a result, many of the better adjuncts no longer wanted to teach in this program, and many of them started to teach at competing programs in the area.

The chairperson realized that she needed to find ways to change the culture of marginalizing adjuncts. Before she could work with the challenge of determining the viability of the academic program, she needed somehow to bring back a number of adjuncts to be part of this process. The chairperson gathered a list of the active and inactive adjuncts and immediately set up a number of one-on-one meetings, a series of general meetings, and a committee that would focus on the assessment of the graduate program and eventually its redesign.

After close to four months of intensive meetings with adjuncts, she was able to form a review committee of nine part-time faculty, headed by the chairperson and assisted by two student research assistants. The chair-person felt that it was important that she chair the com-mittee to signal the importance of its work. Also, the chairperson believed it was important to pay these faculty a stipend for their work on the committee, and, accord-ingly, they were each paid a modest amount. This com-mittee met six times over six months. At the end of this period, the committee approved a program review with recommendations for redesigning the program using an outcomes–based approach. This committee charged the chairperson to form another committee that would actu-ally develop the curriculum for the new courses.

Next, the chairperson held a series of part-time fac-ulty meetings about the changes proposed by the first committee. At each of these meetings, one of the review committee members would be the primary spokesperson about the change. The chairperson would facilitate, but it was evident that the recommendations were the ideas of the part-timers. At each of these meetings, the chairper-son would announce that another committee would be formed that would be charged to develop the curriculum for the new program. The chairperson also sent emails to all of the adjuncts, asking for people to participate in the curriculum. As part of the communication, the chairper-son noted that the committee would be small, with only six members, but that each of these members would lead a group to develop the syllabi. The selected six faculty were paid the equivalent of teaching one course for their work on the curriculum committee.

The curriculum committee, along with the chairperson, met with the school's center for teaching and learning to learn more about designing an outcomes-based program. The center was a critical partner in the program's redesign because of the staff's understanding of adult learning and curriculum design. The group met on Saturdays and Sundays over four months. During this time they first decided on enduring program outcomes (i.e., what learning they wanted their students to have when they finished the entire program). Following from an intentional plan for deep learning, they next determined how they would know their students had achieved these deep understandings. Only after they had achieved these first two steps (determining program outcomes and what would serve as evidence) did they decide on the exact courses, course descriptions, and credit hours for the program. When this work was completed, the information was disseminated to the entire faculty, with a series of intensive meetings to fine-tune the committee's recommendations. At these meetings, faculty were reminded that each of these six members would be heading one or two work groups with the purpose of developing the rest of the new program. A general email invitation to all part-time faculty was sent with a listing of the new course descriptions, the names of the chairpersons of each work group, and contact information for these chairpersons.

After several weeks, the members for each of these groups emerged. In the end, 8 groups were created with a total of an additional 18 new participants (these participants did not receive a stipend for this work) plus the 6 chairpersons, resulting in 24 part-time faculty. These workgroups met over four months to develop syllabi. Each syllabus needed to reflect how the course it represented contributed to the overall program outcomes. By the time the process got to this level, part-time faculty were clamoring to be part of the new program and realized that the faculty who were part of these groups would become the faculty for the new program. The chairperson's role was to make sure that these groups stayed on schedule and to handle any internal conflicts that might arise. At the end of the process, the center for teaching and learning sponsored a public showing of the new program as well as several of the other programs that had gone through a redesign process. However, this redesign process was unique because the part-time faculty accomplished it.

To more closely analyze how the leadership model and the learning model worked together to help part-time faculty emerge as leaders in place, a description of the synergistic relationship between the theories is provided next. Following the explanation of how the models complement each other, the case is revisited, viewed through the lens of this new synergy.

A Synergistic Relationship of the Theoretical Models

A comparison between Heifetz's (1994) model of adaptive leading and Mezirow's (1991) theory of transformative learning quickly leads us to some startling similarities. Both begin by saying that *authority* needs to switch to *leadership*. The person in charge, whether a CEO or a teacher, will need to divest himself or herself of positional authority and embrace a form of shared leadership with the people. Mezirow says they need to become colearners. The leader/learner will mobilize people to do the hard work of adapting and transforming. Secondly, Heifetz distinguishes between technical and adaptive solutions to problems, which is very much like Mezirow's differentiation between instrumental and communicative learning. Heifetz says it is problematic when people confuse the need for adaptive solutions with technical solutions.

Mezirow warns against becoming a "technicist" from only instrumental learning and urges an inclusion of more communicative and transformative approaches.

Third, the way Heifetz (1994; Heifetz & Laurie, 1999) suggests adaptive leading can be fostered is similar to the way that Mezirow (1990, 1991, 1996, 2000) says transformative learning can be fostered (see Table 4.1). As the two ways of fostering leading and learning are compared, it would be tempting to infer steps to take or procedures to follow. However, to do so would be an attempt to instrumentalize a theory that can best be understood with communicative rationality. In other words, as Cranton (1994) indicates, we must avoid the pitfall of creating another set of principles and instead work within a fully informed theory of practice. Therefore, when the interdependent and nonsequential responsibilities for fostering adaptive leading are compared to those same responsibilities for fostering transformative learning, a synergy emerges. The theory of adaptive leading can inform transformative learning theory, and vice versa. As a result of the synergy that emerges between the two theories, the theory of practice for adaptive leading and transformative learning will become more robust.

One limitation of Heifetz's theory is that it does not explain how *individuals* engage in this type of learning. Although Mezirow relies heavily on the notion of discourse and the experience of dialogic exchange for individuals to confront their hidden assumptions and to try on new beliefs, the actual learning process he describes takes place primarily within the individual, not necessarily within the group, organization, or society. Thus, Mezirow's theory complements Heifetz's theory, providing an explanation for how to help individuals learn in deep and meaningful ways. This is critically important for organizations, because "organizations learn only through individuals who learn. Individual learning does not guarantee organizational learning. But without it no organizational learning occurs" (Senge, 1990, p. 139). Leaders lead change by planning purposeful learning in ways that help individuals confront hidden assumptions, embrace disorienting dilemmas, and find new ways of understanding, valuing, and perceiving the world.

The responsibilities for fostering both adaptive leading and transformative learning are compared in Table 4.1, and the synergistic relationship between the two theories is demonstrated in Figure 4.1. In the next section, the synergy is described as it was practiced in the case of empowering part-time faculty to become leaders.

Analyzing Leading and Learning in the Case

Responsibility 1—Go Deep

For Heifetz, going deep means helping people distinguish between technical problems and adaptive challenges. The typical way to handle a program redesign is for full-time faculty to collaborate on defining the goals of the program and deciding which courses would help students achieve those goals. Those decisions would then go to the chairperson and on to the academic policy body that supervises curriculum approvals. After this there would be a meeting with part-time faculty to describe the changes. This process of redesigning the curriculum would be a technical solution to the problem at hand: a solution already understood for a clearly defined problem, being applied in a new situation. Furthermore, it would have been, in some sense, much easier and quicker than the yearlong redesign effort the chairperson undertook. However, she resisted the temptation to make the quick fix and took the risk to embark on a process that would go deeper, that would include part-time faculty, and that would hopefully reap greater dividends of part-time faculty agreement and participation in the process.

In fact, the real problems that existed beneath the surface of the symptoms were not readily identifiable;

Table 4.1. Fostering Adaptive Leading and Transformative
        Learning

Responsibility	Heifetz on leading	Mezirow on learning
1) Go deep	Go beyond technical solutions to help people identify the adaptive challenges	Go beyond instrumental learning to help learners cultivate communicative competence
2) Be patient with distress	Regulate distress. Provide comfort by keeping people within an energizing discomfort work zone, pacing their work, and sequencing their issues.	Be empathetic when learners experience a disorienting dilemma. Model critical reflection of presuppositions and premises.
3) Attend to needs	Create a holding environment for disequilibrium. Gauge the ripeness of strategic issues.	Create a protected learning environment with conditions of social democracy. Block out power relationships.
4) Monitor the process	Give the work to the people, and move back and forth from the balcony to observe. The people must do the work. because it is their beliefs, values, and behaviors that must change.	Use strategies to aid individual reflection and to build a community of discourse. Keep pace with their thinking processes. The learners must do the work of premise reflection, because it is only as they reflect that they will be able to transform.
5) Regard progress	Give voice to ideas that may seem unworkable or disorienting. Let all be heard.	Build confidence in learners' new roles. Protect their rights to choose different perspectives.

Source: A Comparison of Theories: Fostering Adaptive Leading
(adapted from Heifetz, 1994, 1999) and Fostering Transformative
Learning (adapted from Mezirow, 1990, 1991, 1996, 2000)

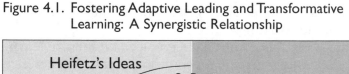

Figure 4.1. Fostering Adaptive Leading and Transformative Learning: A Synergistic Relationship

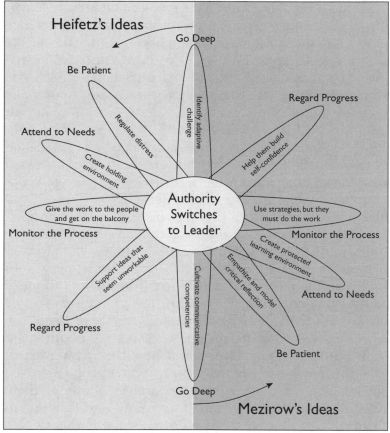

nor was the solution known. In Heifetz's terminology, this was a problem requiring *adaptive solutions*. There was no obvious direction for the master's degree program. Further, there had been previous program reviews and redesigns, but none had addressed the issue of gaining buy-in from the part-time faculty. The chairperson decided to engage the part-time faculty in the process of going deep to discover the adaptive challenges. She knew this process would involve learning—for them and for herself. Therefore, she turned to the school's center for teaching and learning.

This particular center focuses more on faculty learning than faculty training, on communicative competence more than instrumental competence. In order for people to work together to find adaptive new solutions, learning—not training—must take place (Heifetz, 1994). The chairperson knew that for the part-time faculty to make progress on adaptive problems, she had to choreograph and direct learning processes.

Historically, the part-time faculty who had been asked to participate in this program redesign had attended how-to workshops in the school, such as training in how to write syllabi, how to run an interactive classroom and how to deal with difficult situations (e.g., grade appeals). These instrumental types of workshops had created a frame of reference for what to expect when invited to participate in development sessions together. However, in this case the part-time faculty were not invited to learn how to do something, nor were they brought in simply because of their content expertise. They were invited to learn together and to engage in discourse about what their students should learn and how they would learn. The different kind of activity they would engage in posed somewhat of a disorienting dilemma for some of them regarding their role, learning in general, and learning in this program in particular. In order for the part-time faculty to emerge as leaders in the process of finding adaptive solutions for the complex problems of the program, the chairperson and the center staff believed the best approach was for them to come together to learn in communicative, constructivist ways that would shift the focus from how to do things to what meanings they shared with each other about learning and about their discipline.

In order to go deep, the part-time faculty had first to consider what their epistemological views were, what learning theories seemed most appropriate for their students, and how to design a curriculum for evidenced-based learning before they could begin to organize lists of courses, decide on sequences, choose strategies, or pick technology tools. The center for teaching and learning staff was committed to helping these part-time faculty with the deep issues of learning first. The philosophical approach the center takes is depicted in Figure 4.2.

Focusing on meaning is critical to transformative learning theory, because it is the meaning structures we hold that change in the transformation process. Mezirow and Heifetz both speak about learning as change in values and beliefs. Mezirow (1990) says that transformative learning involves reflecting on the presuppositions

Figure 4.2. Faculty Learning Tree

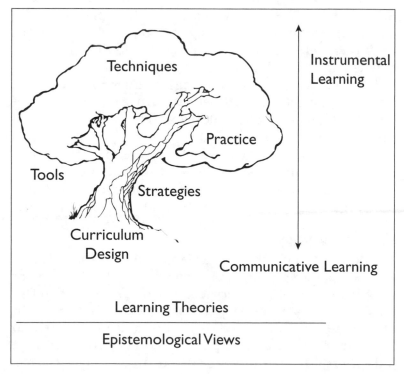

on which our beliefs are based and acting on the new insights, allowing our belief structure to change. Heifetz (1994) notes that through adaptive work, changes in values, beliefs, or behavior take place.

While Heifetz does not seem to require the dramatic shift in consciousness inherent in transformative learning for adaptive leadership to take place, he does seem to suggest that people engaged in serious adaptive work—because they must confront their beliefs and values—may experience the kind of learning experiences that Mezirow describes, shifting their entire orientation to a different way of seeing and perceiving. When this occurs, adaptive solutions can emerge.

Mezirow (1991) differentiates between *meaning schemes* and *meaning perspectives*. Meaning schemes are "particular knowledge, beliefs, value judgments, and feelings that become articulated in an interpretation" (p. 44). Examples of these types of meaning schemes might be the knowledge of a certain academic discipline and beliefs about that knowledge—what is valid and what is not. Other examples of meaning schemes include those habitual expectations governing if-then, cause-effect relationships (Mezirow, 1990). For instance, for the part-time faculty in this case, some meaning schemes they had when they came to the sessions were their knowledge of their discipline, lists of topics they felt the students *should* study, and perhaps a propositional idea that *if* they organized topics coherently and made a sequential plan of courses students should take, *then* the program would be redesigned.

Meaning schemes change more easily than meaning perspectives, which are more like worldviews or paradigms. Meaning perspectives or frames of reference include a "criteria for judging or evaluating right and wrong, bad and good, beautiful and ugly, true and false, appropriate and inappropriate" (Mezirow, 1991, p. 44). There are two dimensions to frames of reference:

a habit of mind and resulting points of view (Mezirow, 2000). People formulate meaning perspectives, or ways of understanding the world, unconsciously in childhood through socialization. These culturally determined perspectives usually remain unconscious in adulthood, but they are very important in determining the way we interpret experience (Mezirow, 1991). An example of a meaning perspective some of the part-time faculty brought into the redesign sessions is the instructional paradigm for an educational program rather than a learning paradigm (Barr & Tagg, 1995). For some, their habit of mind was to focus on inputs rather than outcomes. What would they as instructors teach, what topics should be covered, and what courses should students be required to take?

Not only did the part-time faculty feel somewhat challenged with regard to the learning paradigm, but they also felt challenged in relation to who they were and what their roles were. Meaning perspectives also "determine our concept of personhood, our idealized self-image, and the way we feel about ourselves" (Mezirow, 1991, p. 44). Heifetz warns that when people change the way they see and do things, their self-identity is challenged (Heifetz & Linsky, 2002). These part-time faculty members needed to see themselves as leaders—as experts not only in their subject matter, but also in how adults learn and in how to best design curricula. Because they were asked to go deep, they stayed in their place as part-time faculty, but exercised leadership within their place.

Responsibility 2—Be Patient

Having beliefs and values challenged can cause distress. In this situation the part-time faculty were challenged to think differently about the teaching and curriculum design processes. The new ideas they were hearing pertained to who they were, what their roles were in this work, what they did in the classroom, and how they presented or *delivered* instruction. When they were confronted with the learning paradigm and its implications for curriculum design, some felt disoriented. They knew they were good instructors, and indeed, they would not have been invited to participate in this leading process if they had not been excellent instructors. However, when they were asked to articulate what they do by focusing on student learning rather than instructor teaching, some felt a bit awkward. Would not one assume that if a good instructor teaches, it would follow that students would learn? However, when starting with what their students would learn in terms of deep understandings and how they would know the students had learned, some felt disoriented by the process. Mezirow (2000) claims we either dismiss ideas out of hand that do not fit into our habit of expectation, or we allow ourselves to reflect critically on this *disorienting dilemma.*

According to Mezirow, adults are profoundly influenced by the meaning schemes and meaning perspectives they have developed through years of life experiences. When adults are confronted with a way of thinking that is completely different from what they are used to, if they do not reject it out of hand, they will feel like they have been knocked off their keel. They have had their orientation shaken, hence they have had a disorienting dilemma. The dilemma is to accept the new beliefs and values and allow their perspectives to change or to reject it and to continue with the meaning perspective they already have. The mind works like a sieve—humans sort out what is heard or read and decide whether it should be rejected or whether it will be accepted, and they transform their perspectives.

The new way of thinking in this case was to conceptualize deep learnings the part-time faculty wanted for their students as understandings that would stay with them for five to ten years after they graduated. In other words, they tried to identify understandings they believed would endure even as the world changed. Faculty asked students to write complete sentences to capture what these enduring understandings would be (McTighe & Wiggins, 1999). This is a difficult process in which to engage. Excellent educators often know what they want their students to learn but struggle with articulating that learning as broad, overarching, and enduring under-standings. The part-time faculty could have rejected the process they were asked to use in favor of designing a traditional program with lists of courses, skills, and top-ics, with little attention given to overarching learning outcomes. The process of articulating enduring under-standings created angst for some of the part-time fac-ulty. Thus, it was important for the chairperson and the center staff to support them in the reevaluation of their beliefs about how curricula should be designed, how stu-dents learn, and how they, as part-time faculty, could lead. This was a process that required time for them to reflect critically on their previously held beliefs and val-ues about the teaching and learning process, and about what they wanted the students to learn. The chairperson and center staff needed to model critical reflection for them by asking probing questions in the process. For instance, when the faculty would say that the students needed to learn a certain topic, the center staff would ask them why they needed to learn it. The faculty also needed to be kept energized even though they were in a zone of discomfort, because it is through this uncomfort-able process that adaptive challenges can be identified. The chairperson paced the work, encouraged faculty col-laboration, and kept faculty's focus on the benefits of the new program for the students—successfully maintaining their energetic attitude.

Through this exercise, the part-time faculty began to see how a total redesign of a program could benefit students and faculty. They realized that as they decided upon enduring understandings for the entire program (six emerged), courses could then be designed to help students achieve those understandings. In other words, through the design process of working backward, the program would gain a new sense of coherence, clarity, and consistency. Not only were the part-time faculty leading the development of a new program, but they were also setting an example for other departments to use part-time faculty to lead the way in curriculum design.

Responsibility 3—Attend to Needs

Similar to the disorienting dilemma for the individual is what Heifetz (1994) identifies as "disequilibrium dynamics" (p. 35), a phenomenon associated with the group of people who are engaged in adaptive work. Like people trying to stay on an even keel with their meaning perspectives, social systems under threat try to restore equilibrium, according to Heifetz. The hard work of adaptive leadership requires sustained periods of disequilibrium. When members of the group do not have a ready solution to a problem, they may try to revert to responses from their repertoire. Sometimes solving problems with solutions already known does work, but sometimes people commit an error of the third kind: solving the wrong problem precisely. In other words, if they reverted back to the traditional way of designing the curriculum they would have had a new program, but it would likely not have met the adaptive challenges identified by the chairperson and the focus groups regarding the role of the part-time faculty and enrollment needs. The group needed to be mobilized to produce a new adaptation sufficient to meet the challenge.

Heifetz (1994) suggests creating a holding environment, which he defines as time and space where one party holds the attention of the other party to facilitate adaptive work, regulating the stresses that work creates. Mezirow says that for transformative learning to take place there must be a protected learning environment that demonstrates conditions of social democracy. When faculty work sessions such as these are held over time, such activities can foster communicative and transformative learning (Cranton, 1996). The part-time faculty came together in an informally structured format every couple weeks for three- to four-hour sessions over a period of about four months. To create and sustain a holding environment implies that time is given for participants to reflect and discuss beliefs and values.

Some of the source of disequilibrium came from the passion participants had for their fields, leading to some disagreements over which program understandings were appropriate. As subject matter experts, they represented different areas of expertise, and, at times, there seemed to be some level of competition between these areas. Heifetz (1994) contends that "the clarification and integration of competing values itself becomes adaptive work" (p. 3).

Another source of disequilibrium came from the faculty's vested interest in courses: which courses would be eliminated, which might be combined, what new courses would be created, and who would teach which courses. Mezirow (2000) suggests that facilitators of transformative learning experiences should help "adults learn how to move from self-serving debate to empathic listening and informed constructive discourse" (p. 12). His emphasis is on listening to oneself and to each other, and on helping people to truly hear other points of view. In the same way that Mezirow emphasizes the importance of listening for transformative learning experiences, Heifetz (1994) explains that listening is critical to adaptive leading: "Attention is the currency of leadership" (p. 113). Heifetz's concern seems to be more focused on listening to the issues at hand, which may include the perspectives of others, but which also includes shifting attention away from the technical issues of the situation and directing the discussion to the hard questions of adaptive change. Heifetz also speaks of listening to oneself as a way of gathering data. The chairperson relied upon her ability to listen to herself as she gathered data regarding the redesign process that was under way.

The chairperson had to focus and attend to the needs of the individuals within the group. She knew the strengths and talents of each member of the group and could facilitate the discussions accordingly. She also gauged the ripeness of issues and could determine if the time was right to tackle the issue. For instance, while trying to decide upon evidence of learning, the group began to talk about an electronic portfolio. However, while the issue of determining evidence was ripe, the issue of which tool to use to demonstrate the evidence was not. The chairperson was able to keep the part-time faculty focused on the immediate challenges.

Responsibility 4—Monitor the Process

Throughout this entire process, the leader of the group must move back and forth between the dance floor and the balcony (Heifetz & Linsky, 2002). In other words, the chairperson needed to put herself in and out of the process repeatedly. She needed to be in the process enough to gauge and guide, but out of the process enough to ensure that it would be the people who did the work, that their interests would be represented, and their decisions would be implemented. She also had to make sure that the part-time faculty did not lapse into technical problem solving when the adaptive challenge seemed tough. One member of the group initially wanted to fall back on old ways of doing things—skipping the program outcomes piece and listing topics and skills instead of articulating deep understandings. The chairperson and center staff gently led him to value the process as a group effort that would yield new and adaptive solutions.

Monitoring the process for Mezirow would mean attending to the building of discourse. According to Mezirow (2000), discourse is the process by which the people use an active dialogue with others to better understand their experience and to build consensus. Dialogue is crucial to transformative learning. It is the back-and-forth banter that helps people reflect critically on their presuppositions. If reflection does not come easily for members of the group, there are strategies to help them such as journal writing, critical incidents, and concept maps. The strategy used in this case, to prompt part-time faculty members' thinking about learning rather than teaching, was an exercise in which they were asked to share with the group the best and worst learning experiences they had ever had. The group members listed characteristics of the best and worst experiences on a whiteboard, and they reached consensus about what would make the best learning experiences for their students. The chairperson and center staff monitored the process throughout each session to determine whether strategies such as this one would be helpful. Such monitoring kept them focused on the process, not on a finished product.

According to Heifetz (1994), the people need to do the work, because the problem lies with them; therefore, they must find the adaptive solutions. Mezirow says that even though transformative learning takes place individually, it most often occurs within the context of group dialogue and through the exercise of communicative rational debate. Monitoring the process involves keeping people engaged in the actual adaptive, transformative activity. In essence, this activity is leadership. Heifetz claims that leadership is not a personal set of characteristics or a position of authority. Rather, it is activity within multiple levels of a social structure.

Responsibility 5—Regard Progress

In the same way that Carl Rogers encourages psychologists to use positive ongoing regard when listening to clients (Segal, 1997), the chairperson needed to hold in high esteem the small steps the part-time faculty took toward transformation and adaptation. One of the mistakes leaders and educators can make is to expect the process of adapting and learning to move quickly. They can grow impatient if it does not. Small progress in the right direction needs to be guarded from premature closure or quitting and needs to be regarded as valuable development. In this case, the part-time faculty were told that they would be engaged in work sessions for four to six months among themselves and that afterward they would be assembling their own work groups to flesh out the rest of the courses for the program. It was understood that the group had embarked on a yearlong process. In the long term, it is important to "protect leadership below" (Heifetz & Laurie, 1999, p. 82) to give voice to ideas that may seem disorienting or unworkable. It is essential that all be heard if adaptive solutions are to be found. The chairperson was aware of the quiet voices in the group and made certain they were heard.

Mezirow (2000) states that it is important that the teacher help students to become confident in their new roles and relationships; they may need help with the reintegration of their new perspectives into their lives. The faculty saw support as the outpouring of respect for their work; what they had done was regarded as excellent work in the right direction. The center staff saw the work with the part-time faculty as the beginning of a long-term relationship with this department. They knew that they would hold many more conversations and provide support in a variety of ways, such as through individual discussions on syllabi construction, shared orientation meetings with new students, and explorations of tools to implement the curriculum. Among the key players a sense of team building emerged, trust developed, and respect grew for each other—as educators and as subject matter experts. The process was long, but the chairperson and the center staff guarded progress as it moved along.

Summary

This chapter describes a case in which part-time faculty were empowered to lead their department in the development of a new master's degree program. The chairperson of the department, assisted by the staff of the school's center for teaching and learning, drew from two bodies of literature to inform her practice: adaptive leading and transformative learning.

When the two theories are compared, a synergy emerges that allows each theory to enhance the other. First, as leaders and teachers encourage their people to go deep, they need to search for adaptive challenges and seek communicative learning. Second, they need to be patient with distress, regulating it and keeping people in an energizing discomfort zone, while at the same time supporting individuals who are experiencing the emotional stress of confronting a disorienting dilemma. Next, the leaders and teachers focus on and attend to needs by creating a holding environment for disequilibrium, or a protected learning environment with conditions for social democracy. Fourth, they monitor the process by getting on the balcony from time to time and making sure it is the people who are doing the work, and by helping individuals to engage in critical reflection. Finally, they regard progress by valuing all voices, making sure all are heard—even when ideas may seem unworkable—and by helping people to build self-confidence in their new roles and relationships. When these theories were used together, part-time faculty emerged as leaders.

References

Barr, R. B., & Tagg, J. (1995). From teaching to learning—A new paradigm for undergraduate education. *Change, 27*(6), 12–25.

Cranton, P. (1994). *Understanding and promoting transformative learning: A guide for educators of adults.* San Francisco, CA: Jossey-Bass.

Cranton, P. (1996). *Professional development as transformative learning: New perspectives for teachers of adults.* San Francisco, CA: Jossey-Bass.

Heifetz, R. A. (1994). *Leadership without easy answers.* Cambridge, MA: Belknap Press.

Heifetz, R. A., & Laurie, D. L. (1999). Mobilizing adaptive work: Beyond visionary leadership. In J. A. Conger, G. M. Spreitzer, & E. E. Lawler, III (Eds.), *The leader's change handbook: An essential guide to setting direction and taking action* (pp. 55–86). San Francisco, CA: Jossey-Bass.

Heifetz, R. A., & Linsky, M. (2002). *Leadership on the line: Staying alive through the dangers of leading.* Boston, MA: Harvard Business School.

McTighe, J., & Wiggins, G. (1999). *The understanding by design handbook.* Arlington, VA: Association for Supervision and Curriculum Development.

Mezirow, J. (1978). *Education for perspective transformation: Women's re-entry programs in community colleges.* New York, NY: Teachers College at Columbia University.

Mezirow, J. (1990). How critical reflection triggers transformative learning. In J. Mezirow & Associates, *Fostering critical reflection in adulthood: A guide to transformative and emancipatory learning* (pp. 1–20). San Francisco, CA: Jossey-Bass.

Mezirow, J. (1991). *Transformative dimensions of adult learning.* San Francisco, CA: Jossey-Bass.

Mezirow, J. (1996). Contemporary paradigms of learning. *Adult Education Quarterly, 46*(3), 158–172.

Mezirow, J. (2000). Learning to think like an adult: Core concepts of transformation theory. In J. Mezirow & Associates, *Learning as transformation: Critical perspectives on a theory in progress* (pp. 3–33). San Francisco, CA: Jossey-Bass.

Segal, M. (1997). *Points of influence: A guide to using personality theory at work.* San Francisco, CA: Jossey-Bass.

Senge, P. M. (1990). *The fifth discipline: The art and practice of the learning organization.* New York, NY: Currency Doubleday.

5

Creative Redesign for Change

Mark Hower, Shana Hormann

The Center for Creative Change at Antioch University Seattle celebrated the graduation of its first cohort of students in June 2005 under an innovative new design integrating four master's degree programs. The two authors, Shana Hormann and Mark Hower, are founding faculty in the center. Both continue to teach core courses in the center while taking on additional administrative duties. Hormann is the acting director for the center, and Hower is acting president of Antioch University Seattle. In this chapter, they explore how the faculty overcame initial misgivings about being joined together into an unfamiliar administrative unit and found the inspiration and new curricular design that represented and engaged their collective vision of education for social change.

Designing and adapting course curricula is a common, rewarding, and creative experience in academia, yet the mere mention of redesigning an entire program can bring on a queasy feeling in faculty—even in the most energetic and overachieving faculty. This was certainly the experience of the faculty from Antioch University Seattle's Center for Creative Change as we gathered to listen to an internal review team's report that would change our lives.

The review team, in no uncertain terms, recommended a full-scale redesign of the entire center and its four master's-level professional programs (environment and community, management, organizational psychology, and whole systems design). The team encouraged building on our existing capacity and on what we had in common, and integrating our curricula. However, phrases like "Throw everything into the air and see what comes down" and "Start from scratch" served only to increase the unease of the assembled faculty. In fact, each of the center's four programs had already undergone some form of individual redesign less than a year previously. This sounded much more ominous than a redesign.

The magnitude of the challenge being presented to the assembled faculty seemed too much to take in and accept, individually and collectively, and we immediately began to move through the various stages of grief—with a heavy emphasis on denial and blame. Our former and current students regularly expressed great satisfaction with their education, often stating that their experiences were profoundly transforming. We were using innovative, cutting-edge pedagogy and course content. True, enrollments had dropped, but that was obviously due to an unprecedented increase in competition in just the past few years, a busted economy, and the compounding effect of ever-declining marketing dollars and fewer staff and resources as we did battle every day on behalf of humanity. We felt our hard work was misunderstood and ignored. We were being blamed for the faults and miscalculations of others, from administrators, to marketers, to the world.

Although these sentiments may seem overstated in black and white, it is just this sort of anxious landscape where change runs aground in many institutions. This chapter recounts the story of how Antioch's Center for Creative Change was formed and, more importantly, how its faculty was able to move beyond resistance to embrace the ambiguity of transition and ultimately to join together to transform four separate graduate degree programs into an integrated center. In telling the story, we pay particular attention to the role of faculty, not solely as academics, but as leaders and change agents within their academic setting. For faculty, exercising leadership is naturally interwoven with matters of pedagogy and the curriculum itself. This account of leading in place attempts to express some of the rich possibilities for leadership within a context familiar to faculty.

In the process, telling the story has provided an opportunity for us to reflect on and make meaning out of what often seemed at the time to be random and unconnected events. Several principal themes emerged from the experience, each contributing to the faculty's collective capacity to overcome profound initial skepticism and to design, develop, and implement a thoroughly integrated curriculum. The principles of effective collaborative leadership that emerge from this experience include:

- Deepen collaboration.
- Make leaps of faith in good faith.
- Build collective vision.
- Experiment and build meaning.
- Manage everyday tension.
- Share and embody leadership.

Deepen Collaboration

Systems thinker Barry Oshry (1996, 1999) might have characterized our response to the review team's recommendations as a feeling of being "done to"—a predictable reaction of those on the bottom of a system who feel exceedingly burdened, vulnerable, and put upon by authorities in the hierarchy. It seemed to us in this state that the challenges and problems we faced were coming

from outside of us, someplace "out there"—with "them."
Thus, we perceived that the solutions and responsibilities were also not held by us.

Although these reactions might be normal, we could
not indulge them for long. We had a year to develop
the new design and to begin to implement it. We faced
daunting prospects: the sheer volume of work required
to adequately research options and design new curricula,
the effort entailed in creating syllabi and new marketing
materials, the complexity of teaching an old design to current students while recruiting a fresh batch of students
for the new curriculum. To be sure, these were very real
considerations, requiring significant energy and commitment from faculty who already felt overburdened. However, as Ronald Heifetz (1994; Heifetz & Linsky, 2002)
might categorize the described circumstances, these
were mostly "technical challenges." The effort involved
would be immense, but the kind of work we identified
was known, and familiar solutions were available for us
as experienced educators.

In fact, it was a well-trodden path that had led us
to this point. Just a year earlier, our four programs had
been joined into Antioch's Center for Creative Change,
under the direction of Kristin Woolever. Faculty had
initially interpreted the mandate to form the center as
fundamentally an inspiration of a bureaucratic mind-
set and agenda—not a product of real academic aspi-
ration. In turn, we had approached the challenge with
a technician's sensibilities, so our structural and curricular solutions to the creation of an integrated center were mostly mechanical and cosmetic in nature. The
initial configuration for the center, therefore, consisted
of the four separate programs managed out of one central administrative unit. Each program held its own curriculum apart from the others, retaining its distinctive
strengths and foci. We managed a façade of unity, as we
held regular center-wide faculty and staff meetings, and

our marketing materials and official reports were now combined. But these were rare artifacts, some of the few outward manifestations of our collected but not collective identity. We were still separated by programs rather than joined through them.

It would be fair to say, then, that it was not until the review team told us to "blow up the curriculum" that we began to glimpse the depth of learning and change to which we were being called. Mezirow (1990) describes how transformative learning begins with a "disorienting dilemma" as an experience that creates a powerful sense of disequilibrium such that unexplored assumptions and perspectives are ultimately replaced with new understandings and behaviors. When such profoundly new insights are incorporated into our worldview—individually and collectively—transformative learning and new meaning become possible. But first we had to accept that the curriculum needed to fundamentally change.

The technical challenges we faced, daunting as they were, probably could not explain the visceral responses we felt and were not the biggest obstacles for us to overcome. We would need more than our expertise about human and environmental systems, organizational theories, leadership, design, and the like. We would need to change professionally and personally and move into the realm of the unknown into places where we were not always expert and where we could not control the conversation and experience of change. We would need to embody change itself. Such challenges, without known paths or solutions, or worse, challenges that were not yet fully perceived, are what Heifetz (1994; Heifetz & Linsky, 2002) terms *adaptive challenges.*

We gradually began to recognize that the real challenge was about much more than university politics or budgets or yet another configuration of our courses, organized and taught in essentially the same way with new titles and updated materials. The challenge was within each of us as individuals and as a team. We would need to rediscover ourselves and our identities. We would need to reconsider the true meaning and potential of collaboration, of how students learn, and of the very nature of our faculty roles. In order to manage the stress of being in such ambiguous circumstances, we would all, collectively, need to contribute to the "holding environment" that made it possible to move forward productively.

One fundamental element shared from the outset by each program and each faculty member was our pride in and sense of responsibility to Antioch's historical commitment to engaging with and building a more just society. Every Antioch graduation since the 1850s has included the statement by Antioch College's first president, abolitionist and educator Horace Mann: "Be ashamed to die until you have achieved some victory for humanity." In contemporary language and practice, this principle tends to be about encouraging students and faculty to make a positive contribution to humanity from a place of deep connection rather than from a sense of shame. As a result, social justice, student-centered learning, engaging in reflective practice, and honoring diversity are foundational to pedagogy at Antioch University Seattle. These values are evident in course content and attention to learning styles.

Individually and publicly, the faculty in the center expressed confidence in these shared values and commitment to our students. Privately, we were not always as confident about one another as educators and colleagues. We simply did not know each other, and more than that, we did not really know how to work together. Faculty culture can be, of course, famously individualistic in nature. Jon Wergin (2003) asserts:

> The professoriate is rife with ironies; surely one of the most puzzling is why a community of people who are all committed to a life of engagement with

learning could be so unengaged with each other, or
with the department to which they belong. (p. 41)

This irony was not entirely lost on us, either, as the
importance of creating a learning community within the
classroom had long been a hallmark in several of the
programs. Fairweather (1996), among others, attributes
the lack of a robust team identity among faculty to a
variety of reasons, including a long academic tradition of
rewarding and recognizing individual faculty contributions to the discipline and academy over the collective
contributions of faculty to their institutions and even
departments.

Many of us had experience teaching and working in a
student-oriented community, but we had not, to a great
extent, yet experienced or mastered the faculty counter-
part at an individual program level, much less at the
level of complexity required to collaborate effectively with
faculty from four programs. Collegiality and colleague-
ship are frequently cited as concepts that distinguish
faculty relationships. However, these notions were poor
substitutes for the profound collaboration and commitment to shared responsibility and purpose that would be
needed for our programs to become truly integrated.

Moreover, we had been preoccupied with forming
the bare outlines of the center; we had not sufficiently
engaged in building our own community and knowledge
of each other. The landscape that remained unfamiliar
was not merely around the academic expertise we each
brought to the center or our roles as colleagues. Even
more fundamentally, we did not know each other as
whole persons. We had not built true relationships, along
with the trust and teamwork that can come from them.

In addition to the expected meetings and retreats of a
redesign process, therefore, we began a variety of activities to explicitly learn about each other. We met in each
other's homes to talk about our collective work and to

share food. We held a series of lectures and seminars open to the school and community, but ultimately we were our own audience. One of the faculty interviewed the others about what we most cared about and gathered the transcripts on the web site. These interactions all had an *appreciative inquiry* (see Cooperrider, Sorensen, Yaeger, & Whitney, 2001) sensibility about them, as we were discovering what each and all of us did well and valued highly, without concentrating on what was problematic. We even held a retreat using an appreciative inquiry summit format (Cooperrider et al., 2001) to explore our most powerful experiences of learning and working collaboratively in academia, with the intention of identifying the key principles for our success as a center. Finally, our regularly scheduled faculty meetings included time for sharing experiences related to teaching and learning. We presented high points and struggles and slowly began to build on one another's expertise.

Make Leaps of Faith in Good Faith

Long before we began to perceive the irony of what was essentially an unchanging Center for Creative Change, the new path ahead was being prepared. Myles Horton and Paulo Freire (1991) observed the deliberate and organic nature of change. They might have noted, as they witnessed the faculty's initial work together, that we had to "make the road by walking." Thus, when stories about the early days of the center are retold, it is noteworthy that the actual creation of the physical office space is recounted with great emphasis. Although a seemingly insignificant logistical matter, it was clearly an important point in our formation as a team. In fact, perhaps the first easily identified, overt manifestation of the center came from the simple need to locate the faculty and administrative offices in one office area rather than in four scattered subunits. The chosen locale of the new Center for

Creative Change would be in the already cramped, labyrinthine space of the management and the environment and community offices, dubbed the "Rabbit Warren." The organizational psychology and whole system design faculty and staff would somehow join us. It was a perfect metaphor for the way many of us felt at the time: constrained, overburdened, and undervalued. Conventional wisdom went something like: "Add one more person or desk, and the gravitational pull will create a black hole right there in the middle of the campus!" Astrophysicists might be amused, but we clearly were not.

Nevertheless, we needed to do something, because this would be our home turf into the future. We understood that the space itself would inform how we worked together and connected with each other. One of our team, Farouk Seif, is a gifted architect, and he helped us begin to look beyond the current office layout and what was problematic about its constricted space, toward what would be optimal in our future—somewhat in keeping with a design and an appreciative inquiry approach.

We decided that we wanted a couple of common areas and offices with glass doors surrounding each. The status of having an office with a window as compared to one without would be shared as natural light from outside windows spilled into the common areas through the glass doors. These simple design features would create an expansive living and working space welcoming of a collaborative, integrated approach.

Next, we chose to assign offices in such a way that program groups would be intermingled. The symbolism was obvious, but the consequences were perhaps less so at the time. We were declaring to each other and anyone else who cared to notice that the Center for Creative Change was a united, single entity, no longer a loose collection of partitioned programs. We believe we have the most inviting space on campus to date.

A Quantum Leap: Design

A few months after moving into our shared space, while the sense of our community and identity within the center was also being built, two consultants from the Future Search Network facilitated a three-day conference, A Quantum Leap Forward: Designing the Future of the Center for Creative Change, held October 28–30, 2002. This large group intervention was designed to have the whole system interacting in one room, so we could search together more broadly and deeply than could happen among faculty, staff, and students in the Center for Creative Change. Participants from Antioch University Seattle included a wide representation of students, faculty, administrators, and alumni. Representatives from nonprofit organizations, small businesses, and the corporate sector were also present.

The participants identified 13 common themes as critically important for the future of the center. These included: community collaboration, pluralism and globalization, and transformative process/integration of theory and practice with a subcategory of the theory and practice applied to real world. Special emphasis was given to the creation of a transdisciplinary and intercultural curriculum. In the end, probably the biggest effect of the Future Search Network involved the faculty's perception of ourselves and our role in the change that was being asked of us. As we heard from the varied constituencies, we began to recognize that change was inevitable, perhaps even desirable, and that, in the end, we needed to be the primary engines of that change and the authors of the new curricula. During a memorable small group exercise with the center faculty, we achieved the kind of clarity that is essential for moving forward. We could choose to engage with intention and energy in the work of creating a new center, in putting form, substance, and sweat into the change we wanted in the world. Or we could watch our four programs, our enrollment numbers, and our influence over deeply held aspirations diminish over time.

William Bridges (1980, 1991) notes that transitions are not fully traversed when endings go unacknowledged. Beginnings require endings, and surely our meeting with the review team and the subsequent interactions with the Future Search Network constituted the end of our programs as we knew them and a call to action to design a more integrated, imaginative approach. Freed from the certainty and structures of the past, we could reconsider and reinvent more fully and dramatically.

One week later the center faculty gathered for a day-long retreat to start the work of developing an integrated curriculum. The retreat was ably facilitated by Antioch's dean for university-wide programs, Laurien Alexandre. Although we had much work to do, there was also a sense that we were ready. We could work together as a team on this endeavor that was so central to our purpose and identity. We could agree to start from scratch, risking several courses and competencies that had previously been considered essential to individual programs. We took Future Search Network elements and articulated key learning areas for the core curriculum. Almost every faculty member had to give up a favorite and popular course or put a beloved concept or theory on the table to be either picked up or discarded by colleagues as we designed the core curriculum. Steadily, the broad outlines of the first-year curriculum emerged.

Just a few months earlier, such actions had not been possible. As Heifetz and Linsky (2002) observed: "People do not resist change, per se. People resist loss" (p. 11). Our creativity had been held back by just such a fear of loss, but the interactions of the preceding months had allowed us to build up trust in each other and faith in our ability to leap into a redesign process and toward an uncertain future—together.

As the retreat concluded, we knew that there was no turning back. Our fears about losing our programs and courses—and ultimately our very identities—had been overcome. The comfort of the familiar was replaced with the uncertainty, excitement, and also confidence that new and even bigger, richer possibilities lay ahead. At the end of the day, we set a timeline for further work on the core courses. The center director, Kristin Woolever, left the meeting saying she felt confident about the day's progress. She did not yet have a detailed plan for how to proceed, but she had "a plan for a plan." This retreat was pivotal in our development as a faculty team. We made the redesign and the curriculum our own that day.

After the core courses were determined, we turned to developing the curriculum delivery model. The plan for the plan envisioned a series of concurrent working committees focusing on specific courses and other areas of the curriculum that would need sustained attention. Each faculty member took an assignment on at least two of these committees. While we engaged in this focused work, we also had to consider the broader picture of the whole curriculum and our roles within a truly integrated center. How could we design for program integrity, academic rigor, organizational efficiency, and faculty sanity? Our goal was to build on our strengths and increase our resilience as a faculty team. Three characteristics of resilience reflected our process: facing down reality, meaning making, and ritualized ingenuity (Coutu, 2002).

Facing down reality refers to the ability to truly understand and accept the reality of a situation. While some individuals remained focused on the overall vision, others kept opening doors to new possibilities, firmly connected to probabilities, and day-to-day reality. Our collaboration with one another prevented us from moving into denial, including moving beyond our resources.

Meaning making helps individuals build bridges from present experiences to futures of hope; constructing meaning builds resilience and is itself an act of resilience. Our coming together at meetings and retreats created common understanding and made explicit our shared connection to Antioch's values and beliefs, which in turn ensured that our work was aligned with the mission and goals of the institution. We worked hard to stay connected with one another, knowing that isolation could result in fragmentation of the center's culture and in our working at cross-purposes with one another, decreasing our resilience.

Ritualized ingenuity is the ability to make do and be creative with whatever is available within the parameters of established practices. As faculty we are very familiar with having to make do with what is available, and we are very good at improvisation. On the other hand, organizations have rules and structures, the boundaries within which we operate. Kristin Woolever was new to Antioch University Seattle and had extensive experience in higher education administration. She had a natural credibility with other administrators across campus, and this, combined with the authority of her position, allowed her to maintain the rules and structures for the center and provide the supportive space for faculty creativity and innovation.

Build Collective Vision

When we were first brought together in the center, we could have been four nations, not just four programs. We operated as four silos, acting independently, competing fiercely, and always being "nice" to each other. When we held meetings of the whole center our comments reflected our fears: "We don't want to make the center mushy soup; if we're not careful won't everything look the same?" "Should we have only one degree with different emphases? Does that mean one of our programs will be cut altogether or submerged in another program?"

"We are committed to changing the world and looking through a systems lens; is that all of what we offer our students, organizations, and communities?"

Clarity about how the programs are similar and how they are different emerged as we designed the core curriculum in the working committees. These interactions required that we examine our theoretical foundations. We found that all four programs are built on systems theory. From there we shifted to a focus on natural and social systems. As we learned about the theorists and practitioners who inform our work in any one program, we discovered that even when the authors or sources were the same, our program lenses and responses were different. The answer to the question "Graduate education for what?" may be the same—to help our students to change the world and to create more humane and sustainable systems—but our approaches varied within each program. Nevertheless, there was much that united our perspectives, and identifying these elements of connection was essential as we developed a vision of an integrated graduate curriculum.

Curricula

Integrating theory and practice has long marked an Antioch education, so it is not surprising that the center of gravity of the center's curriculum is the Reflective Practicum I and II Seminars (RP1 and RP2). They are the central feature of both years of study and were envisioned and developed by Don Comstock and later refined by Kate Davies, Farouk Seif, and other faculty who have subsequently taught the Reflective Practicum courses. The underlying premise comes out of Donald Schön's (1983) work on reflective practice, in which Schön outlines the critical need for developing a capacity for and practice of reflection. It is such a practice that allows us to learn from and effectively handle the ambiguity and complexity of modern life. Without this skill and the perspective it can provide, we tend to be at the mercy of events, reacting on the stage of life, without the know-how or sense of distance or perspective to move beyond that ever-present feeling that Kegan (1995) describes as being "in over our heads."

The first nine-month cycle (RP1) is affectionately called "home room," because it provides an important community-building component of the experience of the first-year students. This is also where first-year students begin to hone their analysis and inquiry skills and identify their interest areas within their field of study. In addition to the RP1 course, the first three quarters of a student's experience in the center, regardless of the ultimate degree achieved, involve a core set of courses. Although we have modified each course to fit our current experiences, including our sense of the best order and emphasis of content and developmental fit for students, the core courses remain the same as those first identified at that fateful retreat with Laurien Alexandre. They are:

- *Quarter 1:* Communication Design, Systems Thinking
- *Quarter 2:* Critical Inquiry, Global Pluralism
- *Quarter 3:* Transformative Leadership, Ecological Sustainability

The second year of study in each of the programs involves increased emphasis on degree-specific learning. Each degree program has required specialization courses and electives. The other major component of the second year is the Reflective Practicum 2 (RP2) course. This is a capstone course designed to engage students in a nine-month change project in an organization of the student's choice. A master's thesis is also required and is connected to the change project work. At the conclusion of the final year, students share their change project experiences and results through a public symposium.

The design emerged as a limited-residency cohort model, with emphasis on full-time students and an option for students to attend part-time. Team teaching is the norm for the first-year courses and the second-year reflective practicum. Students and faculty participate as a learning community in face-to-face interactions during residencies, study sessions, and online between residencies. This simple and elegant model met our criteria for program integrity, academic rigor, organizational efficiency, and faculty sanity.

Reflection

Once something like a reflective practice is made a central focus of the curriculum and student learning, it invites a similar critical reflection of faculty's own experience and assumptions. Brookfield (1995) recommends exploring one's own practices through four lenses: autobiographical reflection, the students' experiences, perceptions and experiences of colleagues, and additional theory through literature.

Although the initial design work is complete, we continue to gather in small teams and assemble regularly in meetings of the whole faculty to discuss what we are learning through this experience. All four of Brookfield's (1995) lenses are employed in this ongoing reflective process. In retrospect, as we created the new curriculum in our course teams and in center-wide meetings, it is interesting to note our approach, particularly what we did not do. For instance, a common framing question was: "What do the students need to learn?" We did not specifically ask ourselves, "What do we need to learn?" Neither did we inquire deeply into the nature of team teaching. We assumed it was a good thing, but nothing much was explored beyond that. We focused our attention on the question: "What are our core courses?" We did not fully consider or determine, "What is our core pedagogy?"

This may seem surprising given the fact that we are academics, but our experience mirrors much of what the relevant literature would anticipate given the nature of our newly formed team and community. Before we could truly build something bigger than ourselves and our combined individual experiences and vision, we needed to know enough about who each of us was and what each offered to the team and the intellectual ferment. Luckily, before the call to completely rethink the curriculum, we had tentatively begun to forge working relationships across the boundaries of the programs.

Moreover, this experience serves as a reminder that building a collective vision is not a one-time endeavor with a definitive endpoint. Rather, a vision is a living imperative, and this makes building one an iterative process, with ever-emerging understanding and insight that could not have been achieved in the initial inspiration and design.

Experiment and Build Meaning

The Inspiration of Students

The graduate students in the Center for Creative Change range in age from early 20s to 60s, with the majority of the students in their 30s. Most work full-time and are engaged with their families and communities. Our students hold authority; many have formal authority in their work by virtue of positions they hold, as well as informal authority in other settings. These students approach their education differently than younger students who have less real-life experience. They expect to be taken seriously and for their input to be considered.

Nevertheless, during the uncomfortable phase when an integrated center was still an abstraction, our shared work as faculty tended toward an uncharacteristic detachment from our students. In fact, if the truth be told, as we focused our attention on developing a new curriculum, we probably regarded students with ambivalence at best and even with some amount of fear. Perhaps we intuitively understood that the call for a full-scale redesign also called our expertise and our models into question—if not in our eyes, perhaps in the eyes of our students. If change was difficult for faculty, who were at least somewhat in the driver's seat, what tensions and doubts must have been brewing in the minds, hearts, and psyches of the students? From their viewpoint, they were either about to graduate as the last class of their "true" program or worse, about to be "assimilated"—perhaps unwillingly—into the new culture of the Center for Creative Change.

Our students were mostly not involved directly with the early phases in the center's development, partly as a reflection of our own misgivings and uncertainty about the future. Not surprisingly, students expressed a mixture of responses. A few spoke in favor of being able to take advantage of an integrated curriculum and classroom experience that could model a collaborative-learning environment. Many students, however, held doubts that were not easily ameliorated. The most prevalent concerns were about the effect on their already formed peer relationships and the impact on the quality and direction of their degree programs, now subsumed into one center.

Surely Kristin Woolever had more than a few moments of doubt about our ability to manage faculty and student tensions at this point. But she regularly encouraged us to experiment and innovate, and in turn faculty remained committed to moving forward, even if we were not altogether sure where that was. That spirit, however, seemed to be sufficiently clear to help calm the worst student fears. Our commitment to "teach out" the current programs may have helped as well.

In any case, in response to the students who wanted to sample classes from the other disciplines, a few of the faculty opened their courses to students from the other center programs. Two early examples include Shana Hormann's Group Facilitation course and Sadruddin Boga's Innovation and Creativity course. These courses were very well received by the students who were able to take advantage of the new cross-program feature. However, because our different program delivery models and course schedules were in most cases so dramatically at odds, the potential for greater participation and impact was not immediately achieved. It seemed our students, most of whom are professional, working adults, could not easily adjust their busy lives to four idiosyncratic schedules.

Nevertheless, these small-scale experiments in opening up courses offered the faculty critical opportunities to experience the creative potential that comes from interacting with students from other disciplines. On the surface, such experiments seemed small and relatively risk-free, but they may have been essential to our eventual success, because they brought faculty and students, as well as faculty from other disciplines, into new relationships and direct dialogue about the ideas that we held to be most important. This was not exactly team teaching or collaborative curriculum design, but creative sparks were igniting. When attempting a change project, Shepard (1997) simply counsels: Start many fires. We increasingly found ourselves starting many fires of innovation.

Soon after opening courses to new groups of students, some faculty began, tentatively at first, to invite other faculty from one of the other programs to participate in class as a guest. This again exposed students to different perspectives—often in areas that had a familiar ring, but perhaps within a whole new context. Also, the faculty had a chance to see the impact on the students while checking each other out without making a serious commitment to an ongoing professional relationship. They were, in a sense, our courting days. For many of us, it was the first taste of the stimulating possibilities offered through collaboration with our academic colleagues in a unified center.

Occasionally, something more innovative or even bold was attempted. One of the most memorable early experiments involved joining students from the graduate management program and the environment and community program in a single economics course taught by Don Comstock. Whatever the original impetus for this idea, as the first day of class approached, everyone—faculty and students—in both programs began to have misgivings. Visions of volatile classroom confrontations erupted in our minds, the result of combining two incompatible ingredients: management students (most of whom worked in business) and environment students (many of whom were staunch advocates and had a decidedly anticorporate/antibusiness worldview).

The first class did have a few tense moments as each group tried to grapple with preconceptions of the other and with their shared sense that the basic principles held most firmly within their own programs were at risk. At first, the differences seemed to be too great. In one memorable exchange during a small group exercise, a management student well known for his "green" stance could be heard declaring in a raised voice, "I can't believe this, but when I hear you talk, I keep wanting to say: 'but what about the return on investment?'" Moments later, a participant from the environment and community program exclaimed: "It's return on sustainability that I am after!"

By the end of the course, however, the student response was very supportive, even enthusiastic about the new format. Students expressed their appreciation for the concept and each other, stating that they learned more content and more depth by interacting with their colleagues across the supposed gulf between business and environmental interests.

We soon began to create more electives and to encourage students to take courses across the programs. Student feedback indicated that exposure to different perspectives brought by new faculty and students from different disciplines deepened their learning. Over time, students chose more and more often to vote with their feet by registering for class across the disciplines. As faculty got to know each other's courses, expertise, and programs, we realized there were better ways to integrate our course offerings.

Although student feedback about these early adventures was quite positive, students also expressed reservations. Some resented having students in class from outside their program. Programs of study, like all systems, are self-referential. It is natural for students who are comfortable with the old system to compare their experiences and to assume what is changed and unexpected is also not as good. Such responses mirrored the thoughts of the faculty to a much greater extent than we probably could comfortably have admitted at the time. We were each part of that same self-referential system, after all.

Manage Everyday Tension

Resist-Embrace

In telling this story, two seemingly paradoxical responses to change come to the fore: resist and embrace. Resistance is perhaps most familiar, and it includes the withholding and outright fight against anything and everything that constitutes change. Less familiar may be the concept of grace or the embracing of what could be—of a greater possibility. The story of the center is complicated and ultimately more real, precisely because the intertwining of resistance to and embracing of change has been ever present.

One of the first instances of this dance of resistance and embrace, not surprisingly, involved the creation of the curriculum. Whereas course curricula can be routinely modified, expanded, and shifted without significant distress, programs and disciplines are another matter. Whole programs are almost concrete and immutable to faculty, whose professional lives and careers have been so intertwined with them. So the initial center configuration that held essentially four independent programs did little to threaten this tradition and our comfort. However, once we were committed to an integrated model, the sense of personal identity and loyalty to a specific program made it difficult for faculty to fully embrace what joining the programs together could mean. We spoke of maintaining rigor, standards, program and discipline integrity, key courses, and the like. We were sincere, but we could not so easily perceive that these statements and the values they upheld, however valid and real, also represented the call of the status quo, of what was familiar and known. These were the outward manifestations of deep structures and assumptions of our system, what Wheatley (1992) and other systems thinkers call "strange attractors."

Given the natural tendency to identify with one's discipline or program, resisting any change looks and often feels personal. Such a perception may be based on common sense, lived experience, and personal clarity. Moreover, resistance may also represent the reaction of an internalized system of values and beliefs that is socially constructed, but largely unexamined. This unseen influence seems all the more consequential in the fast-paced complexity of our time.

The authors of *Common Fire: Leading Lives of Commitment in a Complex World* (Parks Daloz, Keen, Keen, & Daloz Parks, 1996) recall a conversation with a woman who feels overwhelmed by the complexity and interconnections in modern life. When faced with a cluster of disconcerting news reports about various troubles around the globe, the woman reported:

> "I feel that somehow I ought to respond. . . . So I try to be good and fair to the people immediately around me—my family and my coworkers. Yet that really doesn't seem to be enough. . . . " The woman pauses thoughtfully for a moment, adding: "I think it is harder to be human than it used to be." (Parks Daloz et al., 1996, p. 1)

Perhaps this experience speaks to many of us, for it does seem harder these days to be anything: teacher, student, administrator, leader, partner, and the list goes on.

Another example of this dynamic of familiar things being more difficult is the role of the program chairs over the course of the center's evolution to an integrated form. The four program chairs, including one of the authors of this chapter, continued to serve in much the same administrative role as they had prior to the formation of the center. There were advantages to this kind of arrangement, because the chairs could help manage disruptions to ongoing commitments, such as those involving current students. The role and leadership of chairs may also have helped moderate concerns about being subsumed personally or programmatically. The transition, then, was not so abrupt.

Once the decision was made to truly integrate the programs, however, the existing structures and roles proved cumbersome. Beyond the obvious focus of our attention on the curriculum, other questions remained unanswered. Should the program chairs remain? What would be the effect on the programs if they were gone? How would the university itself perceive and interact with a center with four degree programs but no program representatives?

Inevitably, the role of program chair became a point of tension between continuity and change. The position was a visible symbol of the old structures and patterns of program organization and authority. Moreover, the chairs tended to feel torn between their responsibility to the program of the past and to that of the future, without clarity about what the future would bring. The present, then, was a constant experience of ambiguity embodied in the concepts of resistance and embrace.

From other points in the system, the chairs may at times have appeared to be resisting—even resisting sensible change as a matter of course. Oshry (1996, 1999) explores how roles and positioning in a system can dramatically influence and even dictate the perceptions each group has of the others. Each perspective has its own truth but also limits on truth. The key is to find a way to discover a new way of being together and to relate in new patterns and with different assumptions.

Thus, those waiting for the center faculty, especially the chairs, to forge a new curriculum were surely frustrated by our lack of progress, even as we were asked to be accountable to the old system of individual programs, not a combination of them. Faculty, in turn, were frustrated by the sense that we were being asked to maintain *and* to dismantle the old system while building the new one at the same time. Meanwhile, we had real students in classes, and they required our attention. This is an example of one of the many transitions of the redesign, and we had to manage—individually and collectively—the tension that such complexity brought.

Myles Horton (Horton & Freire, 1991) observes that people change at a fundamental level when the structures that organize their lives and create patterns of behaviors are themselves changed. He explains: "If you want to change people's ideas, you shouldn't try to convince them intellectually. What you need to do is get them into a situation where they'll have to act on ideas, not argue about them" (p. 16). This is an uncomfortable notion, of course, especially when applied to an academic setting where exploring—or arguing—about ideas is precisely what we do best. But the concept does reflect directly on our experience in creating the center.

The chairs gradually came to this assessment themselves, as they began to understand that the systemic qualities of their positions, coupled with the very personal nature of being the one who "holds" the program, made it difficult for the four separate programs to join fully into one integrated center. In a couple of heartfelt conversations, the four chairs—Betsy Geist, Jonathan Scherch, Barbara Spraker, and Mark Hower—decided it would be wise to simply let go and trust themselves and fellow faculty to the care and good grace of each other. Surely this was in keeping with the collective commitment to form an integrated curriculum and center. The change held some personal cost for each of them, but mostly not of a financial nature. Also, it allowed the chairs to return to a full teaching load, which had great appeal.

Share and Embody Leadership

For faculty in the center, sometimes the inspiration for getting beyond the misgivings of things being harder came from learning more deeply from the lessons we were sharing with students. In the transformational leadership course, Mark Hower makes the point that "every moment is a leadership moment" and that individuals have a choice in every moment about whether or not they will provide leadership and whether or not they will follow—and in what ways. There are always opportunities to either contribute to or detract from the team or group's efforts—to advance or stall the shared journey. As Hollander (1984), Rost (1993), and others have noted, because leadership is exercised within relationships, it is ultimately a shared activity and responsibility. The principles of faculty leadership thus apply to individual faculty initiative and collective action, both on behalf of a larger, shared purpose.

The Launch

The first full test of the curriculum and our new faculty team came during the three-day orientation retreat with more than 40 students in September 2003. Up to this point, all of our inquiry, planning, and preparation had gone toward some point in the future, a powerful yet unrealized vision of how we could be and what we could bring into the world. Then, suddenly, the faculty and students were assembled together, and it was time to realize the vision of an integrated, interdisciplinary master's program.

At one point during the first day, the authors were facilitating a session with the entire group of new students. During one of the small-group activities, in which students from all four programs engaged each other with great animation and enthusiasm, we noticed that the rest of the faculty were nowhere to be seen. We left the room to check on the whereabouts of our colleagues. The missing group of faculty was found in the back break room, engrossed in the drama of a tight game of pool! The center director was proving to be a tough challenge for one of the faculty, and the rest were joking and laughing. The relaxed atmosphere and playful spirit demonstrated by the whole group spoke to just how far we had come. There was an ease and confidence in each other—as people, academic peers, and partners in a great adventure. The room was filled with a sense of comfort in our team and with an embodied understanding that we could lead and support each other. The way the students were embracing this new concept was evident to everyone. We were relieved that the students seemed to hold the various perspectives we had come to expect from each program, and they were also able to appreciate the larger context of the four programs combined.

Much work remained, of course. For instance, we had only sketched out the second-year curriculum, and there were students who had chosen to complete the old programs still to be taught. But from that moment, the faculty collectively and finally stepped into a world as the embodiment of the Center for Creative Change.

Leadership Lessons

In looking back at the development of the Center for Creative Change, a number of lessons begin to stand out against the sometimes chaotic backdrop of the entire redesign experience. These lessons apply to formal leadership and to the informal leadership that the faculty exercised individually and in collaboration. Some of the key lessons include:

- *Deepen collaboration.* Build and encourage collaborative leadership throughout the organization or unit. Collaborate—even when, or maybe especially when—it is not a strength or a widely held practice. Support individual initiative within a context of collective responsibility.
- *Make leaps of faith in good faith.* Take leaps of faith; remain open to new possibilities. Focus attention on principles—what is working and moving ahead—rather than on the details of defining and refining and what is wrong.
- *Build collective vision.* Over time, create a sense of a shared future and collectively pursue the realization of that intention. Articulate and continue to refine a shared vision with the commitment that each member of the faculty needs to have a place for his or her own vision in the larger vision while also supporting the whole.

- *Experiment and build meaning.* Emphasize experimentation and creativity in support of key principles and goals. Nurture a spirit of open inquiry, because new knowledge must be constructed to address adaptive challenges and other unexamined notions of reality.
- *Manage everyday tension.* Accept that change includes the unknown and that managing anxiety about ambiguity is essential as a personal and collective practice. Regularly seek to uncover group and organizational patterns, and respond to or intervene in the patterns in ways that build the capacity and resilience of individuals, the group, and the system. Actively engage key stakeholders, and share the responsibility for creating the holding environment that can support exploration and creativity amidst uncertainty and ambiguity.
- *Share and embody leadership.* Create opportunities and experiences for each member to demonstrate leadership and expertise. Support others when they are leading; take your turn, and then let go of the outcome. Be aware and responsible for tasks and relationships as a shared responsibility, held by each member and the collective team—and not simply by a few authorities.

The Future

Two cohorts of students have already graduated from the new curriculum, and a third group has only a quarter to go. The future for the faculty and students of Antioch's Center for Creative Change seems destined to hold greater explorations of the nature and practice of creativity and change. The leadership lessons cited are based on a systemic perspective—a systemic human model—rather than a mechanistic model. A mechanistic model would assume that the heavy work of a curriculum redesign would be a one-time event, or at least a relatively unusual one. This kind of thinking comes naturally, because in a real sense, we are all members of a society deeply imbued with the mechanistic paradigm. However, that paradigm holds assumptions about reality that set us up for resistance to any changes in the curriculum, because we assume that once a substantial change is made, in any system, the machine is fixed, set in motion, and will perpetuate itself with perhaps only minor tinkering. This is not, of course, what happens in a living human system where new information constantly emerges, new relationships are built, creativity bursts forth, and meaning changes. These and other forces are a fact of our learning and teaching environment, and they present a powerful challenge for us when we do not understand this. Curriculum design and redesign are eventually needed and must be ongoing. When this is understood, resistance is less likely, and we experience the changes as expected, fully planned, and life affirming.

The center faculty is already adding another degree program this year, a master's in strategic communication, and yet another degree is in the conceptual stage at the writing of this chapter. Any new degree will take work to develop, but the strategic communication degree fits well into our interdisciplinary curriculum. The open design readily allows for building on whatever emerges. We are working together as a faculty team to create and own this new degree. We have now established the relationships that allow us to understand and appreciate one another's gifts, share responsibility based on strengths, and exercise leadership with confidence.

Acknowledgments

The authors would like to thank *all* the faculty members in the Center for Creative Change from its inception to the present day for their creativity and commitment. They include: Sadruddin Boga, Guy Burneko, Betsy Geist, Don Comstock, Kate Davies, Shana Hormann, Mark Hower, Jonathan Scherch, Farouk Seif, Barbara Spraker, Pat Vivian, Sue Woehrlin, and Kristin Woolever.

We are also grateful to the several adjunct and temporary faculty who helped us during the transition—whether taking on the critical role of "teaching out" the previous curriculum or jumping into the creative ferment of the new one. These faculty include Kimberly Bowen, Susan Cannon, Lorraine Fish, Morgan McCartor, Walt Meldrich, and RoseAnn Stevenson.

References

Bridges, W. (1980). *Transitions: Making sense of life's changes.* New York, NY: Perseus Books.

Bridges, W. (1991). *Managing transitions: Making the most of change.* New York, NY: Perseus Books.

Brookfield, S. D. (1995). *Becoming a critically reflective teacher.* San Francisco, CA: Jossey-Bass.

Cooperrider, D. L., Sorensen, P. F., Jr., Yaeger, T. F., & Whitney, D. (Eds.). (2001). *Appreciative inquiry: An emerging direction for organization development.* Champaign, IL: Stipes Publishing, L.L.C.

Coutu, D. L. (2002, May). How resilience works. *Harvard Business Review, 80*(5), 46–52.

Fairweather, J. S. (1996). *Faculty work and public trust: Restoring the value of teaching and public service in American academic life.* Needham Heights, MA: Allyn & Bacon.

Heifetz, R. A. (1994). *Leadership without easy answers.* Cambridge, MA: Belknap Press.

Heifetz, R. A., & Linsky, M. (2002). *Leadership on the line: Staying alive through the dangers of leading.* Boston, MA: Harvard Business School.

Hollander, E. P. (1984). *Leadership dynamics: A practical guide to effective relationships.* New York, NY: The Free Press.

Horton, M., & Freire, P. (1991). *We make the road by walking: Conversations on education and social change.* Philadelphia, PA: Temple University Press.

Kegan, R. (1995). *In over our heads: The mental demands of modern life.* Cambridge, MA: Harvard University Press.

Mezirow, J. (1990). How critical reflection triggers transformative learning. In J. Mezirow & Associates, *Fostering critical reflection in adulthood: A guide to transformative and emancipatory learning* (pp. 1–20). San Francisco, CA: Jossey-Bass.

Oshry, B. (1996). *Seeing systems: Unlocking the mysteries of organizational life.* San Francisco, CA: Berrett-Koehler Publishers.

Oshry, B. (1999). *Leading systems: Lessons from the power lab.* San Francisco, CA: Berrett-Koehler Publishers.

Parks Daloz, L. A., Keen, C. H., Keen, J. P., & Daloz Parks, S. (1997). *Common fire: Leading lives of commitment in a complex world.* Boston, MA: Beacon Press.

Rost, J. C. (1993). *Leadership for the twenty-first century.* Westport, CT: Praeger.

Schön, D. A. (1983). *The reflective practitioner: How professionals think in action.* New York, NY: Basic Books.

Shepard, H. A. (1997). Rules of thumb for change agents. In D. F. Van Eynde, J. C. Hoy, & D. C. Van Eynde (Eds.), *Organizational development classics: The practice and theory of change—The best of OD practitioner* (pp. 181–190). San Francisco, CA: Jossey-Bass.

Wergin, J. F. (2003). *Departments that work: Building and sustaining cultures of excellent in academic programs.* Bolton, MA: Anker.

Wheatley, M. J. (1992). *Leadership and the new science: Learning about organization from an orderly universe.* San Francisco, CA: Berrett-Koehler Publishers.

6

Leadership Stymied

Victoria Hardy

> On an overcast day in January, in a damp court-
> yard on the campus of Stanford University, busi-
> ness-school students are kicking their legs, doing
> cartwheels, and shouting out names. "Char-
> lotte!" bellows a woman in brown pants and a
> red sweater, as she kicks her legs cancan-style in
> the air . . . no, the next generation of the world's
> business elite hasn't lost its collective mind. (Sit-
> tenfeld, 2000, p. 276)

The students are responding to directions from Stanford University Professor of Creativity and Innovation
Dr. Michael Ray, in his course, Personal Creativity in
Business (BUS G341), a 21-year mainstay of the graduate curriculum in the business school. Ray's course and
his projects also served as the basis for what *Forbes*
called one of the 100 most influential business books of
the 20th century, *Creativity in Business*, coauthored with
Rochelle Myers. It is this book that gave me the framework to manage what all leaders face: difficult times and
challenging personnel decisions. Ray and Myers focus
on developing skills that encourage creativity to flow and
enhance problem-solving abilities. In the course that is
taught at the Graduate School of Business, each student

chooses an issue to confront that has been particularly troublesome in the past: "What is a problem or obstacle that, if solved, would cause an immeasurable change in your life for the better?" (Ray & Myers, 1986, p. 277). Using this approach has been one of the most valuable lessons I learned from this management leader.

It is particularly important to me now, because the institution where I work has recently undergone a major leadership transition. A new president has come on board following the retirement of a 17-year veteran, and she is the first woman ever to serve in that position at our college. We are also engaged in the first institute-wide strategic planning process in 15 years. These are the times that call for good problem-solving skills and leadership strategies that will ensure the continuation of our department's programs and degrees.

The following case study illustrates the type of issues and problems that can emerge in a time of leadership transition and possible solutions (some more effective than others). At the time, I was serving as a junior tenure-track faculty member of the profiled department. As the lowest-ranking person on the university's chain of command but with 20 years of nonprofit senior management experience, I was in a unique position: "powerless," but with experiential resources that could be valuable, depending on the leadership strategy the academic administrators chose. In this case study, I saw first hand how effective or ineffective various leadership strategies and models can be in the academic setting. The challenge to administrators is how to continue to seek a leadership mode that creates a win-win situation and not just settle for what works temporarily. This case study gives some hope for those who keep probing for the longer term solutions.

"MidWestern State University" (a pseudonym, not my current institution) was founded in the 19th century and is the only applied polytechnic school in the state-supported higher education system. It is an under-graduate teaching school, with only a dozen graduate programs out of hundreds of academic offerings serving its 15,000 students. It is the largest academic unit in the university with more than 3,500 students.

In February 1996, after a disastrous appointment and subsequent resignation six months later of a dean from off campus, the vice president for academic affairs appointed an interim dean from within the college, who immediately turned to reorganizing the college admin-istration and healing wounds from the chaotic previous year. In June 1996 the university administration and the Board of Trustees approved the reorganization, which eliminated two administrative positions and consoli-dated five departments into three. The unit that is the subject of this case study is the Omega Program, which is housed in one of the new departments. The admin-istrative head of the new department was an assistant dean/department chair. Each of the four programs in the unit is administered by either a program coordinator or a director (designation determined by prior title). The line of formal authority is thus dean to assistant dean/ department chair to program coordinators or directors.

Unlike the assistant dean, the program coordinators/ directors are not administrative positions. They are full-time faculty, with a half-time release for handling the administrative duties of the unit. They are first among equals, holding teaching responsibilities and manag-ing the various program units, degrees, and certificates. They also do not participate in the annual evaluations of the faculty in their areas, a function that the department chairs and the associate dean (an academic staff posi-tion) handle. The program coordinators are still classified by the union as faculty, not as administrative personnel, which further contributes to the ambiguity of their role.

The posted position description, however, indicated that the program coordinator would be "responsible for providing leadership," and this brought a long-standing tension in the Omega Program to a full and open conflict, the subject of this case study.

After approval of the new organization in the College of Technology, the interim dean began in the summer of 1996 to put in place his new administrative team. After some false starts and problems with the human resources department (HRD) over posting deadlines, the three new assistant deans/department heads were approved in late August. It should be noted that earlier in the summer, when it became apparent that HRD was not going to move on the assistant dean positions as rapidly as had been anticipated, the interim dean had designated his team with interim appointments—with a clear understanding that these were not permanent arrangements and applicants would be given serious consideration. Likewise, the acting administrators then appointed acting program coordinators/directors for each of their respective units, resulting in an entire college of interim administrators.

At that time, the only member of the Omega Program faculty who expressed an interest in the position was the sole full professor in the program and the senior member of the faculty group. This interim program coordinator was appointed acting program coordinator in July and immediately began to work on the administrative issues that needed to be addressed before the fall semester began in late August. When the program coordinator position was formally posted in September, the interim program coordinator submitted his application—the only faculty member from the unit to do so.

Unlike the other administrative appointments in the college, the appointment of the program coordinator involves significant input from the faculty of each unit. The person who holds this position interacts on a daily basis with the faculty and is therefore the closest line administrator to the teachers. The faculty interviews the candidates and votes on their selection, including a ranking of candidates if there is more than one. This information is taken into serious consideration when the appointment is made by the assistant dean/department head with the approval of the dean. Thus the interim program coordinator's sole candidacy was significant, since no one from the other faculty stepped forward to apply.

The Omega Program unit was composed of seven faculty members who taught in two related programs. The faculty of the program unit included six discipline-based professionals, those who were classically trained with a formal education in their field and the remainder degrees achieved via alternate routes (apprenticeship, for example). The seventh person was a management specialist with an industrial background. The group was therefore generally aligned in two camps: the traditionally educated and those with practical experience.

Those differences had fostered dissension over the years, especially in areas of program development and teaching methodology. For example, one of the most contentious members of the group had proposed for several years that a bachelor's degree be created in the discipline currently represented by an associate's degree. He felt that the students needed another alternative to pursue when they finished their two-year program. There had been considerable discussion about this possibility, and finally the college administration approved the engagement of an expert in the field to come in for a day, work with the faculty group, and then make recommendations to the dean about this possible new direction. The disgruntled faculty member did not approve of the person hired for the consultancy, and chose to keep score at a university football game rather than participate in the workshop.

With the appointment of the interim program coordinator in the late summer of 1996, the differences and dissension between the two groups reached a critical

point. The spokesperson for the nontraditional group
sent a memo to the interim program coordinator, copied
to the entire faculty and the assistant dean/department
head, indicating that he "will not attend faculty meetings that are chaired by you," despite the fact that chairing program meetings is a listed duty of the program
coordinator. The memo continued to outline what he felt
were ten years of problems, including being voted out
of the program coordinator position by the faculty some
five years earlier and losing out on the department head
position, for which he had applied.

The new assistant dean/department head discovered
after some investigation that he had no authority to direct
a tenured faculty member to attend program meetings.
According to the faculty union contract, the only requirements for continuation of employment for tenured faculty
were teaching and advising. Because the assistant dean/
department head was a retired military officer, this particular development was quite disconcerting to him. He
expressed his reaction in numerous informal conversations with individual members of the faculty over the next
three weeks. Based on the advice of the interim dean, the
interim program coordinator did not formally reply to the
memo and was directed to ignore the lack of the disgruntled faculty member's presence at program meetings, at
least until the interim program coordinator was formally
appointed to the position. At this point, the assistant
dean/department head asked for confidential comments
from each of the faculty members regarding the interim
program coordinator's candidacy for the permanent position, in accordance with standard hiring procedures. The
replies to the request were kept confidential.

The vote from the faculty regarding the interim program coordinator's selection as the permanent program
coordinator was thus split; no other tenured faculty
member was willing to stand as alternative, so it became

clear in the first week of November that the interim program coordinator would be selected. At that point, the very unhappy faculty member issued a new flurry of memos on a variety of topics. Since he had not been attending the weekly program meetings, this method was his only recourse to expressing his opinion to the other members of the faculty and to the assistant dean/ department head. When the interim program coordinator's appointment was officially announced on November 12, the discontented faculty member issued a three page memo outlining what he felt were the real issues behind the dissension in the faculty group. Other faculty members clearly felt that some sort of impasse had been reached and that the working relationships had degenerated to a very difficult stage. Consequently, the assistant dean/department head called a meeting of the faculty.

When the assistant dean/department head walked into the conference room on the afternoon of November 14, 1996, he knew that not only did he have a significant problem to confront, but he was also working with his first major challenge to his leadership as a department head. In analyzing this situation, he might well have looked at several theories of organizational behavior to assess the situation and try to determine the focus of his remarks to the Omega faculty. When managing "knowledge workers," a designation that faculty certainly qualify for, it is well to recall exactly the parameters of this kind of employee:

> One can never be sure what the knowledge worker thinks—and yet thinking is his specific work; it is his doing . . . The motivation of the knowledge worker depends on his being effective, on his being able to achieve. If effectiveness is lacking in his work, his commitment to work and to

> contribution will soon wither, and he will become
> a time-server going through the motions from 9 to
> 5. (Drucker, 1966, p. 4)

Even though these observations were written more than 40 years ago, they still hold true.

Drucker (1966) continues with his description of the knowledge worker as someone who does not create a product, in the 19th-century, industrial-age vision of the worker. The knowledge worker produces "knowledge, ideas, information. By themselves these products are useless. Somebody else . . . has to take them as his input and convert them into his output before they have any reality" (Drucker, 1966, p. 4). A better definition of a faculty member at a modern university could not be drawn. The assistant dean/department head could also look to the faculty union contract for legal definitions of what he could and could not do with this group, but his basic instincts told him that he had to face the realities of people whose product is their motivation and challenge in the classroom. If not motivated, an entire program could be lost for lack of enthusiasm in the teaching role, and the talented younger faculty in the program would be susceptible to offers from other universities where the atmosphere might be more collegial.

In *The New Realities* Drucker (2003) acknowledges that "we do not know how to measure either the productivity or the satisfaction of the knowledge worker. But we do know quite a bit about improving both" (p. 113). He outlines the approaches that are key to managing the knowledge worker:

1. We know first that the key to both the productivity of the knowledge worker and his achievement is to demand responsibility from him or her . . .

2. But at the same time, knowledge workers must be able to appraise their contributions [and they] may indccd not always be measurable. (p. 114)

Drucker (2003) would also tell the assistant dean/department head that "placement is key to their productivity. The first rule is that opportunities have to be staffed with people capable of running with them and of turning them into results" (p. 115). The assistant dean/department head knew that the new program coordinator could be an effective administrator based on his experience. But in this hostile atmosphere, would he be able to function in this role and keep the program a contributing asset in the college?

It was also clear that for a variety of personal and professional reasons, the individual faculty members were not willing to confront either of the two lead players in this drama. The long-tenured faculty had been working with and around the personnel differences and problems for many years and were tired of the hassle. They simply did not want to face either of the two warring faculty in meetings or even in the hall. The tenure-track faculty had even more at stake. In the college tenure process, the candidates are ranked by vote of the tenured faculty of their program, then their department, and then the entire college. Becoming involved in a fight between two tenured faculty members was definitely a no-win situation.

If the tenured faculty had been so inclined, they might have chosen to use the model outlined by Fisher, Ury, and Patton (1991) in their ground-breaking book, *Getting to Yes: Negotiating Agreement Without Giving In*. They describe a four-step method that "permits you to reach a gradual consensus on a joint decision efficiently without all the transactional costs of digging in to positions only to have to dig yourself out of them" (Fisher et al., p. 14). The four steps are:

1. Separate the People from the Problem.
2. Focus on Interests, not Positions.
3. Invent Options for Mutual gain.
4. Insist on Using Objective Criteria. (Fisher et al., p. 15)

Fisher et al. also address the question of what to do when the people *are* the problem. They recommend that you build a working relationship independent of agreement or disagreement; you must negotiate the relationship just like any other issue on the table; and you must distinguish how you treat them from how they treat you. "There is no need to emulate unconstructive behavior" (Fisher at al., 1991, pp. 158–159). It was clear, however, that no one in this group was willing to attempt even the first step in effective negotiation because of the people problems. The tension was so bad that some faculty members were avoiding the program meetings for fear of another high-level emotional confrontation.

The assistant dean/department head might also have wanted to avoid the problems defined in Mintzberg's (1983) "professional bureaucracy." When Mintzberg wrote *Structure in Fives: Designing Effective Organizations* in 1983, *professional bureaucracy* was the term he attached to the structural configuration most common in universities, hospitals, school systems, and other public agencies: "All rely on the skills and knowledge of their operating professionals to function; all produce standard products or services" (p. 189). He argues that it is at best difficult—and probably impossible—to effectively manage professionals who are dysfunctional in their work environment. Mintzberg flatly states in the conclusion to this chapter:

Change in the Professional Bureaucracy does not sweep in from new administrators taking office to announce major reforms, nor from government technostructures intent on bringing professionals under their control. Rather, change seeps in by the slow process of changing the professionals—changing who can enter the profession, what they learn in its professional schools (norms as well as skills and knowledge), and thereafter how willing they are to upgrade their skills. (p. 213)

Short of waiting for either of the two antagonists to retire, the assistant dean/department head's options seemed to be somewhat limited, particularly given how universities really function.

In *Organizational Design,* Jeffrey Pfeffer (1978) describes the "coalition" organization, and uses the university as a model:

A coalition model of organizations posits that coalition participants must receive inducements from belonging greater than the contributions they are required to make. Coalition members, then, are continually calculating whether to remain in the organization, or whether they might fare better if they altered their participation. (p. 5)

He argues that "who controls the decisions and actions taken is important because of the differences in preferences and values" (p. 5) in a coalition organization. Pfeffer then describes four bases for influence in the coalition organization:

1. the possession of or ability to control critical resources;
2. the control of or access to information and information channels;

3. legitimacy of the desired position or actions; and

4. formal authority, as derived from the formally designated organizational structure and constitution. (p. 198)

With this information, the assistant dean/department head could have adopted a cynical viewpoint. He controlled the budget for the program, special allocations for travel, approvals for attendance at conferences, and appointments to college committees. He could have chosen to exert his formal authority as the assistant dean/department head and basically to tell the faculty group to work with the new program coordinator or suffer the consequences. However, the realities of working long term with tenured faculty members who also have other spheres of influence in the university and college would argue against adopting such a stance.

Finally, the assistant dean/department head might want to look at the personalities involved in the dispute and see if he had any options for solutions in that arena. According to one model, the DiSC Dimensions of Behavior, there are four possible personality styles that may exist in the group:

D **Dominance:** motivated to solve problems and get immediate results; tends to question the status quo; prefers direct answers, varied activities, and independence; determined and assertive in meeting their needs through direction of others; may be decisive at one end and defiant at the other.

I **Influencing:** motivated to persuade and influence others; tends to be open and verbalizes thought and feelings; prefers working with people rather than alone; tends to be entertaining and motivated to interact with others; may range from invigorating to indiscriminate.

S **Steadiness:** motivated to create a stable, organized environment; tends to be patient and a good listener; prefers participating in a group rather than directing it and listening more than talking; tends to approach problems in a slow steady manner; can be resistant to change.

C **Conscientiousness:** motivated to achieve high personal standards; tends to be diplomatic and carefully weighs pros and cons; prefers environments with clearly defined expectations; tends to be precise, reserved, and concerned with the appearance of conditions; can range from being contemplative to critical. (Carlson Learning Company, 1996)

In this setting, persuading the individuals to undergo the personality test may be difficult, but not impossible. However, with the detailed information in hand about the personality styles, some assumptions could be made. In fact, the new program coordinator had taken the test and had emerged as a D; the profile of a D also appears to fit the other player in this drama. Based on the information about the style mapping material, the limitations of the various types also seemed to apply to this situation. A frustrated high "D" might:

- Overstep prerogatives
- Act restlessly
- Stimulate anxiety in others
- Overrule people
- Be blunt and sarcastic with others
- Sulk when not in the limelight
- Be critical and fault finding
- Be inattentive to details, logic

- Be dissatisfied with routine work
- Resist participation as part of a team

Based on this list, the assistant dean/department head might well have decided that he had a frustrated high D on his hands in the person of the nontraditional faculty member. These characteristics fit much of his behavior over the previous five months, and may be indicative of more challenges to come. There is no doubt that with two high Ds in the small group, alternative ways of achieving harmony needed to be explored. After three decades in the program, the possibility that one or the other might shift from his style was slim. And yet for the group to begin to function, significant change must take place.

The options for managing this group seemed then to fall into three categories: application of formal authority, changing the styles of the members of the group, or changing the composition of the group. The assistant dean/department head basically chose the first alternative: His meeting with the faculty on November 14 was very direct and to the point. He announced the interim program coordinator's appointment as the program coordinator for the next two years and invited the members of the group to figure out a way to work together—or else. The meeting was brief, blunt, and unproductive. But it was clear that the assistant dean/department head expected some action on the part of the faculty. In effect, he had exercised a more traditional form of leadership, based on his military experience rather than on information about managing knowledge workers. At this point, Ray and Myers's (1986) admonition became relevant to at least two members of the group: "What is a problem or obstacle that, if solved, would cause an immeasurable change in your life for the better?" (p. 277). These two individuals decided that a different form of leadership needed to happen and took responsibility for the next stage of this dilemma. The goal was to significantly change the group so that the work of the program could proceed.

At that point, the two faculty conferred and presented the option of a strategic planning session to the group. Specifically, they proposed to use the services of a faculty member in the College of Arts and Sciences who was a specialist in conflict resolution. This colleague was someone with whom both antagonists were willing to work in this environment. It took more than a month to get the group to agree on a date and an agenda. The facilitator also agreed to privately interview both parties about their roles in the meeting. Everyone had to agree to allow him to facilitate the meeting and to abide by any decisions that the group would reach at that session.

The resulting meeting was held on the last day of the semester. Several important decisions were reached that day that did seem to alleviate some of the dissension in the group. First, the program coordinator agreed to relinquish chairing every program meeting in favor of an alternating chair. He was to be given an opportunity at the beginning of each meeting to present any program-related items from his meetings with the assistant dean/department head, but the chair would set the agenda for the meeting. His opponent agreed to attend all the meetings, even those chaired by the new program coordinator in his rotation. The faculty also voted to table further discussion of any program changes until the enrollment figures warranted expansion into another degree.

The new semester began with this operating agreement in hand. It was not easy, and there were a few strange encounters, but the program meetings proceeded in a reasonably functional manner. The system began to fall apart in the late spring when the hiring process for a new faculty member began. The posturing and negative aspects of the two high D personalities in the group again emerged. Fortunately, the group was able to achieve consensus on three of the six finalists, which gave the assistant dean/department head a decent field of people from which to select a candidate. The addition of a new faculty member to the group would certainly change the dynamics again, hopefully for the better. In the meantime, the new program coordinator would continue for at least one more year, at which time the whole process could be revisited.

When managing knowledge workers, administrators and executives must increasingly use what Drucker (2003) calls the "liberal art" of management. Merging actions and applications of theories to find solutions to complex situations will continue to be a challenge for the best of managers. It requires the utilization of not one, but at least two tests of applications to find those parts of the art of management that will work. Drucker (2003) also reminds us, however, that

> The single most important thing to remember about any enterprise is that results exist only on the outside . . . The result of a school is a student who has learned something and puts it to work ten years later . . . Managers who understand these principles and function in their light will be achieving, accomplished managers. (pp. 230–231)

As the new leadership takes the reins at my current institution, lessons to be learned from these past experiences are myriad. Primarily, in times of transition, it is important to remember that old alliances and new partnerships will merge. As the former leadership is replaced with senior administrators in support of the new president, one must be vigilant and aware of the challenges of leadership in times of change. Keeping your wits about you, listening to colleagues, and thinking outside the box will all serve as important tools. Creative solutions to leadership will be needed to persevere in times of change.

References

Carlson Learning Company. (1996). *Personal profile preview 2.0* [Brochure]. Minneapolis, MN: Author.

Drucker, P. F. (1966). *The effective executive.* New York, NY: HarperCollins.

Drucker, P. F. (2003). *The new realities* (Rev. ed.). Somerset, NJ: Transaction.

Fisher, R., Ury, W., & Patton, B. (1991). *Getting to yes: Negotiating agreement without giving in* (2nd ed.). New York, NY: Penguin Books.

Mintzberg, H. (1983). *Structure in fives: Designing effective organizations.* Englewood Cliffs, NJ: Prentice-Hall.

Pffeffer, J. (1978). *Organizational design.* Arlington Heights, IL: AHM Publishing.

Ray, M., & Myers, R. (1986). *Creativity in business.* New York, NY: Broadway Books.

Sittenfeld, C. (2000, June). The most creative man in Silicon Valley. *Fast Company, 35,* 276–279.

7

Sharing Leadership in an Academic Health Center School of Nursing

Carol A. Reineck

Leadership is difficult to define, but exhilarating to practice. In their elegant work on organization behavior, Gibson, Ivancevich, Donnelly, and Konopaske (2006) discuss several theories of leadership because no one theory seems to be fully representative and adequate. Bass (1990) defined leadership as:

> an interaction between members of a group. Leaders are agents of change, persons whose acts affect other people more than other people's acts affect them. Leadership occurs when one group member modifies the motivation or competencies of others in the group. (p. 21)

This definition includes ideas such as influence, change, and accomplishing goals. Shared leadership, then, seems to incorporate the simultaneous notions of sharing influence, sharing the process of planning and implementing change, and accomplishing mutual goals.

The Department of Family Nursing Care is a thriving academic department at the University of Texas–San Antonio Health Science Center. It is one of three departments in the School of Nursing within the large academic health center. Shared leadership lives there. As interim chair, I encouraged all of us within the department to share influence, lead change, and accomplish mutual goals. The department is well known and respected within the academic health center as large, bustling, and productive in the three core pillars of teaching, research, and service.

Here is the tale of the manner in which an entire academic nursing department, not just I as interim chair, shared in department leadership by engaging together to conduct a comprehensive self-assessment program. The mandate from the executive vice president of the academic health center directed that each department engage in a self-assessment program followed by an internal review. In this instance, "internal" meant internal to the academic health center but external to the School of Nursing. As interim department chair, I chose to transform a hierarchical requirement into an opportunity for horizontal, participative leadership by the faculty. Shared leadership was the way the project was accomplished. The evaluation itself was just one outcome. Other outcomes included the priceless commodities of faculty satisfaction, esteem, and the honor of having shared in the leadership of the department.

This chapter begins with a brief description of the department and its mission to prepare nurses for the future. Next, I offer a brief reflection and clarification of how past experience influenced my participative leadership style in the department. The next part of the chapter is a sequence of events and an outline of parts of the process in which faculty leadership emerged and was fostered. An overlay of seven leadership values follows. Each phase of the department evaluation, which linked to one of the seven values, is explained next. Finally, I offer excerpts from sample letters from me as chair and from two reviewers. The excerpts highlight leadership attributes of the department faculty. These letters provided me with the opportunity to communicate and promote faculty leadership success. The communication role of the chair is vital in a shared leadership environment to keep channels of ideas and recognition open. Selected excerpts from faculty-written passages add additional texture to this example of leadership in place.

The Department

The Department of Family Nursing Care faculty members prepare nurse practitioners and teach the nursing care of the childbearing and childrearing family, as well as mental health nursing. They write and conduct major federal grants concerning pediatric, family, adolescent, gerontology, and mental health areas of concern. Faculty advise baccalaureate, master's, and doctoral students. Many faculty engage in clinical faculty practice as nurse practitioners and in other advanced practice nursing roles in hospitals, clinics, and centers in the community. Some from outside the department would call it "high maintenance," referring to the fast-paced, high-intensity interpersonal academic environment made up of strong-willed, busy, and exceptionally capable faculty.

In 2005, the dean appointed me interim chair of this high-maintenance department with a $1.4 million budget. Why was I chosen to lead? After all, I was a faculty member in one department and was invited to serve as chair of another. Here are a few of my thoughts. My participative leadership style was well known in the School of Nursing. In the previous year, I showed interest in the leadership and financial responsibilities of my own department chair. I learned later that my chair recommended me to the dean. Looking back prior to my joining the faculty at the university, my career in the Army made me—and many like me—a leader from the first day on active duty. On my first day as a professional soldier—a first lieutenant—I was appointed assistant platoon leader for my basic officer orientation class. My platoon, made up of 40 brand-new Army Nurse Corps officers from all over the United States, gave me the first of many leadership positions I was fortunate to hold. Others through my memorable 31 years of Army service included head nurse, section director, chief nurse, and deputy commander. The dean knew of my former years of military leadership and was also aware of my demonstrated leadership in the School of Nursing and in the university. These leadership contributions included serving as faculty senator and as an officer in the faculty assembly. When the dean asked me to leave my comfortable faculty office and step up to this leadership position, I surprised even myself. I did not tarry with my decision. I made one phone call, gained encouragement, took a deep breath, and returned in less than an hour to say yes to the dean's invitation to lead at the department level. I greatly respected the faculty and the mission and could not wait to help create an environment where we could unify our efforts and share leadership.

My unexpected appointment came at a time when three important initiatives began. First, faculty members were engaged in a major curriculum revision of four nurse practitioner graduate programs. They were integrating the curricula. This required developing a core curriculum as well as curricula unique to each of the four practitioner programs. Second, faculty made a decision to transform a significant part of instruction from a face-to-face to a web-based delivery system. The purpose of that decision was, in great part, to improve access to graduate education for nurses in rural Texas and those living in under-served areas on the U.S.–Mexico border. Third, the department was directed to perform a self-assessment and internal review during the upcoming academic year.

As interim chair, I could not have come on board at a time that was any more challenging. My charge from the dean was to make these and many other things happen—within budget, of course. I jumped in. Later, after a full year had passed, I reflected. I found that it was not I who made things happen. It was the collective we.

Experience as Influence

My prior experiences as a chief nurse executive shaped my leadership toolbox. Working in major medical centers alongside other professionals, I found that horizontal collaboration and shared leadership were the best management methods in a complex, service-oriented organization. When all members of the organization participated in continuous quality improvement and were invited to share responsibility for patient care excellence and safety, everyone benefited.

Experience in health care and nursing administration taught me many valuable leadership lessons, including: Share everything; put things back where you found them (Fulghum, 2004). Other lessons were to get out of the way (a lesson an Army sergeant taught me years ago), remove barriers, find resources, encourage risk taking, and develop people. In the course of my leadership experience in the Department of Family Nursing Care, these ideas had no chance to collect dust. I used them daily to keep the department humming.

The Department Evaluation:
An Opportunity to Share Leadership

On the day that I was named interim chair, the departing chair said, "and, by the way, you will need to do the department evaluation on your watch." I knew little about what that meant, but I was certain that I could not hide from it. As Hatfield (2004) correctly stated, "There is nowhere for a department chairperson to hide" (p. 1).

I quickly redefined the meaning of "you" in the parting quote from the departing chair. Faculty members in my new department were exceptionally capable in their respective areas of expertise. They had also been members of the department for enough time to appreciate the many valuable contributions of faculty members to the missions of the school. "You" did not have to mean "me." That is to say, the department evaluation and any other major initiatives did not have to be my job alone as chair. It could be—and should be—*our* job. The hierarchical way of getting things done did not fit in the presence of exceptionally capable faculty who showed interest in sharing the leadership.

My previous background as an officer and executive in the Army Medical Department grounded me in core values. I stood on these values through times of turmoil and times of relative peace. Over the years, these values influenced how I perceived the weighty requirement set before me as an academic leader. Not only would I soon be responsible for day-to-day operations of the 37-member academic department, but I would also initiate and guide an extensive evaluation of the department's productivity with regard to teaching, research, and service. I realized that by modeling these values, I could influence people to do great work.

Some readers may view the military in a stereotypical command-and-control frame of reference or paradigm. Examples of this view might include visions of giving orders, saluting, and not questioning authority. But, in fact, the military in our country operates on the successes of small group leadership. The platoon I mentioned earlier is an example of such a group. The small group leader models values and takes care of soldiers so that through soldiers' abilities and motivation the mission is accomplished. In the Army, every soldier learns about leadership. Every soldier has the opportunity to lead. In the university, every faculty member, like the soldier, is a member of one or more small groups and has great potential to share in the leadership when given the opportunity. We need to be about the business of making that opportunity present itself more often.

According to Marchese (1993):

> Educational institutions must monitor the quality of goods and services they provide to be able to improve continuously—which means that people in those organizations must systematically keep track of how the organization is doing and that the resulting information must be readily available to all within the organization. (p. 12)

Marchese was right. The evaluation would be a systematic but long road, beginning with the first phase—organization and planning. I believe it was in this first phase that shared leadership in our department began. Within a rigorous project timeline, faculty participated as leaders in evaluating their own department.

The assessment required collection, tabulation, and articulation of large amounts of data. Table 7.1 summarizes the main areas of the assessment that the committee completed in addition to their teaching duties in less than one academic year. Wergin (2003) made the important point that departments need to "define for themselves the critical evaluation questions" (p. 35) within the context of overall institutional needs and priorities. He further suggested that a flexible and decentralized approach may separate effective from less than effective evaluation strategies. As chair, I made efforts to transform a centralized process, imposed at the executive level in the university, into a decentralized one with significant leadership by the faculty. Faculty members showed leadership to study and articulate the performance of the department. They effectively operated the institutionally determined criteria. By bringing the criteria to life the faculty performed leadership in place.

Table 7.1. Components of Departmental Assessment

Assessment Component	Subcomponents
Elements of Effective Leadership	Continuing education Development Budget Formula funding Infrastructure support Unit leader self-evaluation
Education Activity	Student enrollment and retention Minority enrollment and retention Licensure exam pass rates Faculty profile Education grants New programs
Practice and Service	Practice income and practice grants Work environment Faculty/student interdisciplinary activities
Research	Funding application and acquisition, Faculty/student publications Interdisciplinary activities
Future Challenges	Unfunded requirements Staffing challenges

A Values-Driven Process

The *task* was self-assessment at the department level, followed by internal review. The *process* was one to which I, as interim chair, chose to apply values and shared leadership. Although the charge came from an upper-level academic executive, the evaluation was horizontal—across and throughout the department—and values based. The values that guided the horizontal approach appear in Figure 7.1; they form the acronym LDRSHIP.

As background, in 1998 the U.S. Army initiated programs in character development to place emphasis

Figure 7.1. Leadership (LDRSHIP) Values

Loyalty—faithful adherence to a person or unit
Duty—the legal or moral obligation to accomplish all assigned or implied tasks to the fullest of your ability
Respect—treating others with consideration and honor
Selfless service—putting the welfare of others before your own
Honor—being honest with one's self and truthful and sincere in actions
Integrity—doing what is right, legally and morally
Personal courage—overcoming fears, danger, or adversity while performing your duty

Source: U.S. Army

on the core values listed in Figure 7.1. Using the easily remembered acronym LDRSHIP, the Army integrated these values into new doctrine, training plans, and other programs, including officer and enlisted performance evaluation reports. Interestingly, each of the seven values has a bearing on how faculty in my department were empowered to demonstrate their leadership in completing the evaluation.

An academic department evaluation serves as an example of how shared leadership can be implemented. The seven self-assessment phases and their suggested corresponding leadership values are:

- Convening and organizing the work of the faculty committee (duty)
- Engaging the dean and nursing faculty as a whole (loyalty)
- Identifying and working with sensitive data sources (integrity)
- Working with other offices to share information (selfless service)
- Learning about the department (respect)

- Keeping on target with timelines (honor)
- Hearing and acting on the reviewer feedback (personal courage)

Convening and Organizing the Work of the Faculty Committee—An Example of Duty

The sense of duty refers to "actions required by one's position" (*Webster's Concise American Family Dictionary*, 1999). It is an obligation to accomplish work to the fullest of one's ability. The dean expected me, as incoming chair, to convene the department evaluation committee, give guidance about the committee's responsibility and work product, impose a timeline, and mobilize secretarial and other support. My duties, then, were to convene, charter, and support. Three questions loomed: Whom would I choose to serve on the committee? Would the faculty I selected be willing and able? How would the committee organize itself for the responsibility? These are the kinds of questions leaders need to ask.

First, I considered whom I would choose. Hatfield (2004) reminded chairs that "successful program level assessment is faculty-driven, not driven by top level administration" (p. 5). Even though this project was larger than program level, I chose to employ Hatfield's admonition. Who will know best how well a department is functioning than the faculty who compose it and give it life?

The department that I chair is composed of 37 faculty members. Four are tenured faculty. The remaining majority are not yet tenured and nontenure-track faculty members. Lees and Brown (2004) would concur that a nontenured faculty majority is a norm in staffing academic departments. Tenure status was an important factor in my decisions on committee composition.

In our school, there are two tracks for academic progression: the tenure track and the clinical track. Tenure track is the pathway for faculty who seek to engage in teaching, research, and service over a long period in the university environment. The clinical track is intended for those faculty members whose aim is to remain clinically focused, primarily teaching and supervising students in hospitals, clinics, and community health settings. Rank among faculty members of the department ranges from specialist to instructor to full professor. For the evaluation process, I chose three faculty members. One member, Dr. W., was a senior, tenured faculty member who had recently been promoted to full professor. The second member was Ms. C. D., who had just declared her intention to apply for promotion to assistant professor. The third member was a specialist, Ms. P. D., who had served faithfully on the faculty—teaching maternal-child nursing for more than 30 years.

I designed the composition of the three-member evaluation committee to include one tenured and two clinical-track faculty members. Why? First, it was my intention to add the experience and perspective of a tenured faculty member. Second, I wanted to give an opportunity for leadership service to the clinical-track faculty member seeking promotion. Third, I felt more secure with the time-tested leadership capacity from the remaining clinical-track faculty member, whom I trusted to get the job done well. The mix was exceptionally effective. It yielded three individual faculty perspectives reflecting the variety of experience, leadership, motivation, and organization requisite for this responsibility.

Toward the middle of the committee's work, I appointed an additional member, Dr. R.—an assistant professor on the tenure track whose workload had changed, thereby releasing time to assist with the project. The additional faculty member entered the project well after the committee had formed and departed for another position before the work was complete.

I discovered later that this appointment late in the process was not a good idea. Shared leadership is not always perfect. The late entrance of an add-on faculty member proved to do more to disrupt the process than to enhance progress. I learned, as chair, that it is best not to assume you are helping when you add people to an effort already under way. No matter how good my intentions, it would have been much better to consult with the committee before changing its composition in any way. A faculty member taught me that important and humbling lesson: Assume nothing!

As department chair, my next concern was, would the three selected faculty members be ready, willing, and able to exercise shared leadership? The department chair whom I succeeded suggested that I ask Ms. P. D. to lead the committee. When I called Ms. P. D., I introduced myself as the incoming chair, outlined the project, and indicated that her organizational skills and proven leadership in clinical teaching teams were exemplary. I also indicated that the former chair and I had great confidence in her ability to take the lead on the project.

At first, Ms. P. D. suggested that a tenure-track faculty member should chair the committee. It may have been her perception that leadership attributes required being tenured or on the tenure track. Not necessarily so, I felt. I shared with her that although it is true that tenure-track faculty need to be involved in and lead committees, this particular committee demanded proven leadership, which she had demonstrated many times over the course of her 30 years. Also, having a committee chair from the clinical track offered honor and recognition for the clinical-track faculty members in our school. The clinical track is selected most often by faculty in the School of Nursing; it plays a pivotal role in preparing professional nurses for entry into nursing practice and for advanced nursing practice. Finally, she agreed to my request. She said she would serve. This is an important point about leadership in place: Tenured faculty are not the only ones who should share academic leadership. The inherent leadership attributes of nontenured or non-tenure-track faculty members are valuable resources and need to be mobilized as well.

My duty as interim chair was to properly constitute the committee and begin the process. It was my duty to take the initiative, but I needed the faculty to assume leadership; I believed in their capability to share leadership. The remaining two members were pleased to serve when asked. Their willingness was evident after they knew that the committee leader had been selected first. I learned that selecting the committee leadership first helps greatly to constitute and mobilize the remainder of the committee. Wergin (2003) suggested that "faculty like work that is not only vibrant and intellectually interesting, but work that takes us somewhere" (p. 19). It was my hope, indeed, that the work that lay before the committee would take us somewhere.

Engaging the Dean and Nursing Faculty as a Whole—An Example of Loyalty

Loyalty is the thread that binds our actions together and causes us to support each other, the school, and the university. The process required loyalty to the faculty and to the dean. The department evaluation committee began their work nine months into the administration of a new dean.

As our dean noted, "At first, you are called 'the new dean.' Then you are called 'the dean.' It is only much later that a dean is called, 'our dean'" (Dean Robin Froman, personal communication, January 22, 2004). The committee began the process, then, with the new dean in place. The new dean fully supported this process with information and insight; she concurred with the composition of the committee and the timeline to accomplish the responsibility. This is another important point for leadership in place. When there is harmony in the way

deans and department chairs view faculty empowerment, faculty leadership can more easily flourish.

As chair, I met with the committee to give them their
charter, timeline, and to offer departmental support. I
informed the dean, associate deans, faculty members,
and department staff members that the committee was
convened. The purpose of the notification was to garner
their cooperation in advance for that time when the committee would ask them for information or support. I tried
to pave the way and to prime the institutional pump.
Then I stepped out of the way.

Loyalty to the dean meant completing the department evaluation well and on time so that the dean, in
turn, could report the accomplishment to her superiors
in the academic health center. Loyalty to faculty meant
keeping them informed of the progress of the committee
and ensuring that the committee members were aware
of all the respective accomplishments and contributions
of their colleagues.

Identifying and Working With Sensitive Data Sources—An Example of Integrity

Integrity is the basis for trust and confidence that must
exist for an academic—or any other—organization to be
effective. It means firmly adhering to a code of moral and
ethical principles. The department evaluation committee
was entrusted with confidential documentation of faculty accomplishments. The faculty member who capably
served as chair of the department evaluation committee
described her experience with such issues as working
with sensitive data sources. In her concluding comment
in the excerpt below, you will see that she speaks of
being privileged to view information of which she was
previously not aware. She guarded that information with
integrity. Her meetings were always conducted in an environment where faculty information could be protected.

The following passage describes her initial response to being asked to chair the committee, her recommendations for preparing for the next department evaluation, and insight into the need for the department chair to be fully engaged and supportive.

> When I was appointed to chair the department evaluation committee, I was hardly overjoyed! The task seemed daunting. It had to be done in addition to my other responsibilities. Fortunately, our chair also appointed two very capable faculty to the committee and, together, we were able to accomplish our charge.
>
> In addition to the expenditure of time, gathering the data proved more difficult than expected. Summaries of department activities over the three previous years were not uniform and data were not always compiled in a systemic or complete manner.
>
> Based on my experiences chairing this committee, I have a few suggestions which might facilitate the process.
> - Keep yearly summaries of department activities.
> - Appoint a committee that reflects the department's mission and faculty mix.
> - Consult with committee members before altering the committee.
> - Consider workload when assigning faculty to the committee.
>
> Even though I have been on the faculty many years, I did learn a great deal from this process. I came away with increased respect and admiration for several department faculty, whose accomplishments I had been unaware of prior to this evaluation. Our chair was also very helpful to us in completing this assignment.

Working With Other Offices to Share
Information—An Example of Selfless Service

Selfless service is putting the welfare of others before your own. It is the ability to endure hardships and insurmountable odds (Washington Army Guard, n.d.). The committee members kept selfless service in mind as they diligently gathered data from the Office of Graduate Studies, the Office of Undergraduate Studies, the Office of Nursing Research, the department files, the community liaison, and other sources. The committee members were putting the welfare of the dean, chair, and faculty ahead of their own work obligations; they were motivated to work toward the common good because of their commitment to the School of Nursing.

Selfless service among faculty does not result in self-promotion or enhanced personal comfort. While faculty members on the committee gained recognition during and at the conclusion of the process, their motivation was not to gain recognition but rather to serve in an important way and have significant positive impact on the school to which they were deeply committed. Classic writers in turnover research (Hackman & Oldham, 1980) spoke of a related concept: task significance. *Task significance* is feeling that the work one does is important and affects the lives of others. Task significance has been linked to job satisfaction. It is probable that the faculty felt not only selfless service but also task significance. One faculty member, Dr. G. W., whose excerpt appears next, wrote how the committee's labor-intensive work contributed to such significant aspects of the life of the school as curricular decision-making and accreditation. This was an expression of selfless service and task significance.

The tenured faculty member who served on the evaluation committee, Dr. G. W., spoke of the data-gathering effort as "a labor intensive but valuable experience." I estimate that this committee collectively spent more than 500 hours to accomplish this evaluation. Dr. G. W. adds the following thoughts.

> The process of internal review of our department was a labor-intensive but valuable experience.
>   This type of evaluation process can assist both faculty and administrators in decision-making. The process can guide curricular decisions, as well as provide input regarding faculty and staff development needs. Finally this process can help to identify the impact specific educational programs have on the community as well as address outstanding needs related to accreditation.

Learning About the Department—An Example of Respect

Respect is treating others with consideration and honor. It is the ability to accept and value other individuals. Respect begins with the fundamental understanding that all people possess worth as human beings. Respect is developed by accepting others and acknowledging their worth without feeling obligated to embrace all their ideas (Washington Army Guard, n.d.).

Personal information about the faculty was treated with great respect by the committee. Over the course of six months, the committee pored over the curricula vitae of 37 faculty members, identifying their contributions to the various dimensions of the evaluation: leadership, teaching, practice, service, and research. To the great credit of the committee, its members handled all the information in a confidential and respectful manner.

At the completion of the evaluation, the committee chair said that the respect she held for her colleagues increased as she learned more about their teaching, research, and service. Moreover, the committee members learned the dollar value of research funding secured by faculty members. They also became aware of the breadth of private foundations and governmental agencies whose financial support faculty had garnered through their valiant and persevering efforts in grantwriting.

When I learned of the degree of surprise about accomplishments and the deepening respect among faculty for each other, I realized that as an academic leader I could foster that respect still further. I could increase mutual awareness of faculty accomplishments. The School of Nursing started a newsletter titled *The Tribute* during this time period. We were able to enhance communication of faculty contributions through this newsletter, thereby building respect and esteem among the faculty. Shared leadership creates an environment in which all are valued for their strengths.

Listening to Others' Points of View—An Example of Honor

Peter Drucker (2004) was once asked, "Which of your twenty-six books are you most proud of?" (p. x). Drucker, then age 85, snapped, "The next one" (p. x). The next one was *The Daily Drucker,* in which he suggested that "to know one's strengths, to know how to improve them, and to know what one cannot do—are the keys to continuous learning" (p. 26). Drucker admonished the reader to revere feedback and listen to others' points of view in order to continue to learn and grow. Honor, in a shared leadership environment, carries with it elements of honesty—being honest with oneself, being truthful and sincere in actions, and respecting feedback to improve.

Toward the end of the first three months of the evaluation process, it appeared to me that committee members were ready for me to begin to mobilize internal reviewers. The committee members and I were prepared to honor others' points of view, which would be made known during the internal review. We respected the chairs who agreed to serve as reviewers. We knew their expert feedback, gleaned from their experience and insight, would improve our final product.

At the time of her departure, my predecessor suggested individuals by name who would serve capably in the reviewer capacity. I appreciated her suggestions and began to contact three faculty members—all chairs—who could serve as internal reviewers. I sent a letter to each of the three reviewers. The letter honored their expertise; it also honored and paid tribute to the extensive work of the faculty committee who had labored for months. I invited the reviewers to serve. I held my breath, and they said yes!

In a shared leadership environment, communication of faculty members' efforts to outside scholars is an important way to gain feedback upon which further growth and insight can occur. Scholarly work, when peer reviewed (as in this evaluation process), brings honor to those who produce, support, and review the work. Together, the committee and I lifted up a compilation of the contributions of the entire faculty in the department to be reviewed. In so doing, we honored their individual and collective work.

Hearing and Acting on Reviewer Feedback—An Example of Personal Courage

We are familiar with physical courage—the ability to overcome fears of bodily harm while performing a duty. Certainly fire rescue personnel show personal courage when they enter burning buildings to save lives. Moral courage is overcoming fears of other than bodily harm while doing what is right even if it is unpopular—Rosa Parks refusing to give up her seat comes to mind. Still another kind of courage is personal courage—candidly taking what may be considered by others an unpopular stand (Washington Army Guard, n.d.). The reviewers demonstrated personal courage by rendering candid reviews of the quality of the self-assessment document. The reviewers did not seek to be popular with the committee members. Likewise, the faculty committee members

showed personal courage when they left their comfort zone and entered into candid discussion with reviewers about the quality of their extensive work product. They did not know the comments were going to be positive and expressed some apprehension before meeting with the reviewers. Also, they had a great personal investment in the product. After receiving a compliment, the dreaded word "however" can signal the beginning of useful feedback. Internal Reviewer B demonstrated use of the dreaded "however."

> I was very impressed by the many department/ university and extramural activities and accomplishments of the faculty. *However*, it was difficult to assess the temporal achievement of goals within specific timelines. In other words, what goals were set for each faculty member and what projected milestone(s) were to be used for evaluating satisfactory performance ratings?

All three of the internal reviewers were department chairs. Two offered candid feedback in written form. The third reviewer, Internal Reviewer C, gave a candid verbal report that clearly recommended a complete reformatting of the final product. It took personal courage to listen to and accept the constructive verbal feedback. The committee could see new ways to present the product in a manner that would be more readable and tailored to the goals of the department instead of adhering to a standardized but not meaningful format suggested by the executive suite.

It is important to note that Internal Reviewer A mentioned that faculty in the department helped achieve department goals while contributing to areas in which they were each uniquely qualified. The reviewer perceived that faculty were participating in leading and accomplishing the work of the department. Reviewer A's comments

were generally quite positive. In contrast, Reviewer B made more use of a mix of positive and constructive feedback, which took somewhat more courage to receive.

Reviewers A and B personally presented their honest and open reports to the committee. Committee members stated that they were apprehensive about receiving the reviewers' reports. Overcoming fear, the committee members demonstrated personal courage by listening carefully to positive comments regarding what they had done well and to constructive ideas regarding areas of possible improvement (the "howevers"), which included better explication of the budget and greater attention to the match between faculty goal setting and goal achievement. Reviewer C, who gave her report to the committee verbally but not in writing, was especially frank. She suggested that the committee rethink the format of the final evaluation report and not be tied to a standard format. The committee felt a sense of liberation in that they could create the report in a manner that best articulated the productivity of their department, emphasizing the ways faculty leadership in the university and community was shared among all.

Faculty reaction to the constructive criticism was one of openness. The members of the committee had never engaged in such an arduous process before. They allowed themselves to be in a learning mode and took copious notes as the feedback with criticism was being delivered. They wanted to meet right away to act on the suggestions for improvement and create an improved format. In a shared leadership environment, I communicated to faculty members that I had the greatest of confidence in their ability and ideas. As a committee, they indicated to me that they appreciated this kind of support. Leaming (1998) emphasized that a department chair can keep morale up by working to create a supportive culture:

Do what you can to provide an environment and structure that adequately satisfies the human needs of your faculty and encourages new ideas, risk-taking, and creativity. It should be an exciting, reinforcing environment that encourages faculty members to engage in professional activities and meet new challenges. (p. 134)

I, too, wanted to stand up and speak honestly about the work of the committee. As the department evaluation was nearing conclusion, the committee members were very anxious to be discharged from this task! As department chair, I wanted to recognize their efforts in a number of ways. I acknowledged them publicly in a department meeting, highlighting their efforts, and I asked that they be honored with a hearty round of applause. I placed a copy of their final department evaluation in the lobby of the department so that others could openly view their work and respond to it personally. Finally, I sent each of them a letter of thanks. Leadership in place provides many opportunities to thank faculty for their contributions to leading the school.

Summary

In the life of an academic chair, many things are inevitable. One is that a department chair is in a strategic position to provide leadership opportunities for faculty. An example of such an opportunity was performing a formal evaluation of departmental functioning. The department evaluation—conducted by the academic health center department's empowered faculty committee, which I convened—served as a valuable opportunity to share the leadership within the department. It was a model for other departments and for the school. Leadership values, including loyalty, duty, respect, selfless service, honor, integrity, and personal courage—which form the acronym LDRSHIP—formed a conceptual overlay for the evaluation process.

The point is that shared leadership involves creating an environment in which faculty, with their inherent personal strengths, embrace the work of the entire school. Living the aforementioned seven leadership values may enhance the warmth of that embrace.

Individual faculty members who participated in the evaluation process expressed, in their narratives, that they encountered barriers and facilitators. Barriers included lack of availability and completeness of data, format requirements, unwelcome addition of a committee member midway through the work, and simultaneous teaching workload. Facilitators included support and communication from the department chair.

Committee members made several recommendations. First, they recommended that the chair of each of the three departments in the School of Nursing keep yearly summaries of department activities. Second, the chair should consult with the committee before altering its composition. The chair should realize that assumptions made about helping the committee may be erroneous. Never assume anything! Third, the chair should exercise care in determining the mix of committee members, making sure that most disciplines and specialties are represented to the greatest extent possible.

My Reflections

Leadership in a complex academic department, when shared with the faculty, results in greater productivity, growth, and satisfaction. Major initiatives such as curriculum change, teaching delivery system change, or departmental evaluation provide excellent opportunities to engage the full participation of the faculty.

The process of evaluating the productivity of an academic department works in concert with values. These values offer a framework upon which one can shape this important and inevitable process in the life of an academic department. The process cannot and should not be separated from the values that surround it—such as the importance of integrity when assimilating sensitive information and honoring the strengths of faculty.

Three well-chosen faculty members led the evaluation of their department in an academic health center. I assembled and charged the committee and then—to empower them—I stepped aside, except for times when barriers needed to be removed or resources acquired. I created a positive leadership environment founded on values, in which committee members understood the mandate and their duty and operated with wide latitude and generous support. As a result, committee members learned and gained satisfaction, honor, and esteem from leading the process. Scholars such as these committee members who remain open to constructive feedback from reviewers earn the intrinsic rewards of professional growth, respect and acknowledgement from colleagues, and an opportunity to work in an academic environment in which leadership in place can flourish.

Acknowledgments

I acknowledge the contributions of faculty in the Department of Family Nursing Care for their commitment to education; Dr. Joel Baseman and Dr. Terry LeGrand for their expertise in academic leadership; Dr. Robin Froman, dean of the School of Nursing, for her guidance; and Dr. Nancy Girard for mentorship about how best to lead as a department chair. Ellen Nathan provided professional editorial assistance. My husband Todd, himself a leader and teacher, encouraged me.

References

Bass, B. M. (1990). *Bass and Stogdill's handbook of leadership: Theory, research, and managerial applications* (3rd ed.). New York, NY: The Free Press.

Drucker, P. (2004). *The daily Drucker: 366 days of insight and motivation for getting the right things done.* New York, NY: HarperCollins.

Fulghum, R. (2004). *All I really need to know I learned in kindergarten: Uncommon thoughts on common things* (Rev. ed.). New York, NY: Ballantine Books.

Gibson, J. L., Ivancevich, J. M., Donnelly, J. H., Jr., & Konopaske, R. (2006). *Organizations: Behavior, structure, processes* (12th ed.). Boston, MA: McGraw-Hill/Irwin.

Hackman, J. R., & Oldham, G. R. (1980). *Work redesign.* Reading, MA: Addison-Wesley.

Hatfield, S. (2004, February). *Implementing assessment on the program level.* Paper presented at the annual meeting of the Academic Chairperson's Conference, Orlando, FL.

Leaming, D. R. (1998). *Academic leadership: A practical guide to chairing the department.* Bolton, MA: Anker.

Lees, N. D., & Brown, B. E. (2004, February). *Staffing academic departments.* Paper presented at the annual meeting of the Academic Chairperson's Conference, Orlando, FL.

Marchese, T. (1993). Total quality management: A time for ideas. *Change, 25*(3), 10–13.

Washington Army Guard. (n.d.). *The seven Army values.* Retrieved September 7, 2006, from: www.washingtonarmy guard.com/values.html

Webster's concise American family dictionary. (1999). New York, NY: Random House.

Wergin, J. F. (2003). *Departments that work: Building and sustaining cultures of excellence in academic programs.* Bolton, MA: Anker.

8

Following the Leader and Leading the Followers

Joseph Barwick

Discussions about leadership usually appeal to only a small segment of the employees of the college community. True leaders are a minority, if not rare, and followers are not usually inclined toward analysis of the magic that compels them to be led. On the other hand, most employees are, in fact, in charge of something. Teachers are in charge of students, courses, and curricula; researchers are in charge of methods, labs, and grants; administrators are in charge of whatever their roles dictate; and most other staff are in charge of oversight for processes, equipment, or something else deemed necessary to the organization. Why is it that when most people are in charge of something, we still think of leadership as an attribute of the few?

The answer, of course, is that there is a qualitative difference between managing and leading, and the literature on leadership over the past four decades is thorough, if not ponderous, on the distinctions between the two (Bennis & Nanus, 1985; Hersey & Blanchard, 1982). What is not clear in the literature, however, is the defining point at which an excellent manager should rightfully be considered a leader, and likewise, the point at which a leader ceases to be one because he or she cannot manage. I explore that elusive point in this chapter, recognizing that, like so many things in science, reality is more a function of perception than of absolute nature.

As Jon Wergin pointed out in the opening chapter of this book, more people within the organization need to cross over into the realm of leadership and aspire to be better at it, and the ones in leadership positions need to better understand its qualitative difference in order to encourage and nurture it. The colleges and universities that are going to move into the forefront—to become leading institutions—are those that have deployed leadership throughout the organization rather than localized it in positions of formal authority (Gardner, 1987). Great institutions must pull together, bringing together all the creative and intellectual capital they have. The ones that fall behind will be those made weaker by the growing rifts between faculty and administration, students and faculty, and other competing divisions within the academy.

The literature on leadership is quite extensive in its array of definitions and lists of attributes associated with successful leaders. This literature is presented in other parts of this book, and I do not attempt to review that again. Instead, I take what might at first appear to be a simplistic view of the subject and invite readers to connect it to their own professional positions, experiences, and perceptions of how best to use leadership for personal or organizational advantage. For me, "leading" implies three basic, underlying assumptions: that the leader is going somewhere; that others are going there, too; and that they are going there because of the leader. This explication of leading is deceptively simple because of the various behaviors that are often associated with the concept but that do not fit.

Leaders Do Not Lead in Place—They Move

The ability to influence others is a necessary component of leadership, but influencers are not necessarily leaders.

Influencers, sometimes called opinion leaders, can shape opinions and sometimes even organizational culture, so they have a great deal of power. However, they typically do not have a sense of direction so much as a position on the issue of the day. Because of their critical thinking and communication skills, they can see ramifications of issues that others might have missed, and thus they can be highly persuasive. At their worst, these are the people in faculty or dean's meetings who can tell everyone all that is wrong with an idea, but they rarely offer viable alternatives. If their motives are personal, such as simply deriving pleasure from the power to persuade, they are a negative force, and any leader who wants to accomplish something must learn to work around them. On the other hand, if they truly want to separate good ideas from the bad and are capable of supporting a direction or goal that advances the mission of the institution, they are tremendous assets and resources. Leaders will seek these people out, often informally, to gain access to their points of view as well as to garner their support before they begin to exert influence in another direction. (Kanter, 1983)

The leader, in my simplified definition, is going somewhere, not merely trying to influence opinions (Kouzes, 1988). The leader might be going somewhere transactional: that is, trying to gain something or avoid losing something, such as pay, better benefits, or more control of curriculum. Or he or she might be going somewhere transformational, such as becoming a learning college, a premier research institution, or a leader in international education. When looking at leading this way, it is important to note the potential danger in the motives of the leader. Leadership, regardless of its point of origin in the college, should help pull an institution together, not advance any narrow agenda. For example, R. W. was a senior math professor who was elected president of the faculty in the early 1980s. This role gained him a seat on the president's cabinet, and he was expected to provide the voice of the faculty on a day-to-day basis. At that time the college had a few computers placed around the campus, but technology was not used extensively in classrooms or offices. The president moved in a bold direction and committed significant resources to make the college a leader in the use of technology. R. W. was a Macintosh user and took it upon himself to make sure the college adopted an Apple platform. He vehemently criticized any alternatives that were not Apple, lobbied faculty and department chairs about the limitations of others, and did exhaustive research to support his preference.

In the end, the administration chose to adopt a PC platform but allowed the math department and the art department, the only two who specifically requested it, to go with Macintosh. The point here is that for the year in which this controversy raged, the faculty had virtually no voice in administration. R. W.'s sudden singularity of purpose did not represent the faculty, because most of them did not know enough about computers for the differences to matter. What the faculty did want to discuss was the impact computers would have on learning, how integration of technology might affect curriculum, and how this commitment of resources might affect other pressing capital needs. These things, however, were not discussed, and other matters of concern to faculty that emerged in the president's cabinet were no longer of any concern to the faculty's elected president.

True leaders know more than just what they think, believe, or want; they also know where they are going (Schein, 1992; Bennis, 1989). Contrary to this is the protester. Anyone at all familiar with the concept of civil disobedience is well aware of the importance of protest in a free, democratic society. A person who has the clarity of insight to see that a policy or practice is too odious to be allowed to continue—and has the personal charisma to get others to join in the effort to stop it—is, in truth, a leader. However, this action is taken only after the rifts and dissension have become so great that no other actions can effect change. Because the underlying assumptions about leading used in this chapter are based on the premise that leading, in the college-wide context, can prevent such rifts, I will say no more about leadership whose sole purpose is to prevent opposition.

The concept of advancing as being integral to the definition of leading cannot be overstated. Even when leading in a transactional direction (e.g., to gain a better compensation package for faculty), a true leader will be concerned about how this objective, if accomplished, will impact the ability of the larger institution to advance as well. A person elected or appointed to negotiate on behalf of faculty would be remiss not to work aggressively in their best interests. However, for a leader to know where he or she is going, the leader must be able to see beyond the signing of the final contract and into the future of the college (Kouzes, 1988). A resolution that weakens the college is not in the best interests of the faculty, regardless of the short term benefits. The leader in this position has the added burden of not only advancing the goals of the faculty but also advancing the health of the organization by influencing faculty to embrace compromises that might be necessary (Schein, 1992). The group looks to the leader for guidance on the whole trip, not just the destination.

This is even more important when leading in a transformational direction, because in this case, the trip is without end. J. S. was promoted to vice president of administration of a small, two-year college following a person who had held the job for more than twenty years. The previous vice president managed by intimidation, played favorites, and pitted work groups against each other. As a result, morale was low, and the division was plagued with gossiping, character assassinations, and finger pointing. Although faculty and staff frequently complained about this division, payroll was always on time and accurate, environmental systems functioned reliably, and there was never an audit exception.

As an employee of the college, J. S. took the position because of the challenge of changing the culture and climate of the division while maintaining or improving the level of performance. She began by having individual meetings with each of her subordinates, in which she explained her expectations for the division, not the individual employee. These expectations included the division working together as a whole rather than as competing work groups. She also discussed the destructive social behaviors and made it clear that these would no longer be acceptable. Through all these interviews, J. S. remained confident in her new status as "boss" and did not try to solicit their support as a peer based on her former position. Her role as vice president gave her, not the employees, the authority to determine the direction the division would take. It would take leadership, however, to actually move in that direction. The elusive point between management and leadership in this case was J. S.'s ability to focus her employees on a meaningful horizon beyond their specific job (see Pascale, 1985). Annual climate surveys showed a rapid and dramatic increase in job satisfaction of the employees; and in program review surveys, this division now gets consistently high marks from other employees for their customer service. Not only has there been no drop in performance, but the division has achieved greater efficiencies and has saved the college money. Leadership, in this example, was clearly effective, but because the direction was transformational, it did not end. All the leadership behaviors that caused the division to turn in the right direction must be continued for that direction to be maintained. One does not trim the sails on a ship once and expect it to stay on course forever (Kuh & Whitt, 1988; Tierney, 1988).

Without Followers, Leaders Are Just Out for a Walk

The second basic assumption in this concept of leadership is that others are following the leader. Because this is a necessary component, good leaders have usually been good followers themselves (Hollander, 1987; Kelley, 1992). The leader-follower relationship is formed around an objective that is larger than the needs of either entity. The leader needs the followers in order to reach the objective, and the followers need the guidance, encouragement, and vision of the leader. In other words, leading cannot exist outside the leader-follower relationship.

In academic organizations, leading generally falls into two categories. The first is protecting the interests of one group against the competing interests of another. Faculty often feel in competition with administration, because they do not believe the allocation of resources supports what they do (i.e., teaching and research). Likewise, administrators often believe that faculty are stuck in traditions that impede the progress of the college. Because this rift is so common in academia, leaders in both camps easily take on these oppositional ideologies, and communication becomes strained at best. R. H., president of a large southern college, had a management style most would describe as autocratic. He had very strong opinions about the mission of the college, the value of students, the importance of technology, and even about how to teach. As he was not inclined to keep his opinions to himself, he was openly critical of traditional forms of teaching, in particular the lecture method. Needless to say, the campus began to polarize. R. H. was the founding president and, therefore, had followers who supported him with almost fanatical zeal. On the other side, however, were faculty who were quite successful teaching in ways the president seemed to criticize. Anyone in an academic environment can readily see the multitude of issues at stake here and the potential for an ever-widening division that could eventually bog down the entire college.

A good leader, however—and this is essential to the leader-follower relationship—has enough confidence in his or her own goals and direction not only to allow dissenting opinions but to encourage them (Stout, 1984; Ouchi, 1981). To R. H.'s credit, he sought out opportunities to engage in dialogue with teachers he considered traditional, and he encouraged a strong faculty senate, meeting weekly with representatives of the faculty. Gradually, another group of followers began to emerge. These faculty recognized that R. H.'s criticism of traditional methods of teaching came from a combination of his value for student learning and his belief that every teacher had an obligation to students and the college to constantly seek a better way to teach. New informal leaders arose, who enjoyed experimenting with ways to improve learning, and as they gained recognition within the organization, the dialectic about traditional teaching became less visible. Under R. H.'s leadership, the college gained national recognition for being one of the most innovative colleges in the country. R. H. had the authority to compel faculty through various forms of censure and reward. Instead, he chose to effect change through open debate (see House, 1971). The new faculty leaders who emerged could easily have moved into the camp of the traditional teachers, but instead they chose to listen more closely to what the president was trying to say. In doing so, they discovered that the apparently competing interest of the traditional faculty (i.e., autonomy in the classroom) was never really in jeopardy. R. H. wanted innovation. As long as he had it, others were free to do whatever worked. As with most successful organizations, the credit for their success is due as much to the informal leaders—the committed followers—as to the president (Kelley, 1992).

The second category of leading is in aligning the interests of one group with those of another (see McGregor, 1960). Colleges have missions, values, and goals, and every employee of the college should support those or have the courage to seek employment with a college whose mission, values, and goals he or she can support. That said, however, there is plenty of room for debate and dissent over specific initiatives, policies, or edicts. It is important, however, for leaders to always be aware of whether they are leading in the direction the college is going, even if they disagree on how to get there. Except in very rare instances, leaders within and throughout the organization cannot lead a college away from the direction established by the president and the board. Efforts to do so are extremely costly in terms of lost energy and creativity. For example, J. B. became head librarian shortly after the installation of a new president. The previous president had enjoyed technology and had invested heavily in making the library a showcase in terms of computers and electronic research. The new president brought a strong message of renewed community focus. He wanted the college to be inviting to the community while at the same time finding better ways to meet the needs of the students. J. B. realized that most of the community patrons avoided the high-tech resources in favor of print and that students usually wanted more personal help with their projects. Working through the dean and eventually the president, J. B. phased out some of the less-used technology and increased holdings in the periodicals. She paid attention to what the community patrons checked out and moved these materials into more prominence with better access. As hiring opportunities occurred, she looked for interpersonal skills above computer skills, believing correctly that the latter could be more easily learned. In a fairly short period of time, use of the library by students had greatly increased, and more than one-third of the patrons were from the community. J. B. had the skills and the choice to continue to grow the library as a state-of-the-art, high-tech learning resource center, but she determined that a shift back to a more traditional library would move the college forward along the path the president had set, and she led in that direction.

J. T. became dean of instruction under a president who had been at the college only three years. The fairly new president had brought much-needed organization and structure to the college, based primarily on the concepts of total quality and continuous improvement. The employees bought into these methods, because they saw that issues were being assessed and problems were being addressed. Successes were evident and celebrated, so morale was also rising. Where the faculty balked, however, was over the president's approach to student learning through "customer focus." These faculty were having trouble thinking of students as customers, because it lessened the students' humanity and put teaching in the same category with selling used cars. J. T. realized that energy was being wasted over vocabulary, so he began to engage faculty in discussions about the needs of their students. They discussed what kinds of attendance policies are best for 35-year-old single mothers coming to school at night. They discussed how best to motivate 18-year-olds who have no clue what they want to do. As they discussed, they implemented and measured new processes and services to meet the needs of a diverse student body. J. T. helped the faculty see that providing better service to students is not just a good business model for improving the institution's bottom line, but it is the right thing to do, which they already firmly believed. Once the needs of the faculty to hold on to their humanistic values were aligned with the president's need for a continuous improvement approach, students received better service. J. T. could have been a good manager and simply acted according to the president's direction. Instead, he used his leadership ability to bring the values of the faculty into alignment with the goals of the president.

Managers are accountable for various processes that help an organization accomplish its mission. However, if every manager, from the president on down, does only what is in his or her job description, the organization will still eventually grind to a halt. Throughout the organization there are opportunities to find better ways to accomplish whatever tasks or services are required, and the college needs leaders in these places to move the college forward.

Leaders Make a Difference

The third basic assumption in this definition of leading is that the followers are following because of the leader. That is, without this leader, they either would not go or would go somewhere else. For truly good leaders, followers want to go, because they want to be where these leaders are (see Etzioni's [1961] *personal power*, and French and Raven's [1959] *referent power*). The specific objectives of the direction are less important to them than the association they feel to the leader. Although there are many dimensions to the leader-follower relationship, just as there are many ways to get people to do things they would not have thought to do on their own, it is this desire to associate with the leader that is the most elusive to describe (Bass, 1985).

This kind of leading can be found at any level of an organization, and most people, if asked to name the people on campus who inspire these feelings, could come up with a fairly consistent list. Yet the people themselves are typically more diverse than alike. One thing that is always true in this type of leader-follower relationship, however, is that in some way the leader stands apart from the followers. The person might be kinder, wiser, more honest, wittier, or some other comparative, but in fact this person is not so much like others as he or she is someone the others want to be like. When R. C. rose to department chair after years of being in the department, she thought relationships would stay about the same. As long as she was fair about schedules, allocating resources, and other such things, she did not see any reason why things would be different. However, as she moved in higher circles at the college, she began to see that there were many things her department could do differently and better. In order to accomplish these effectively, R. C. knew her colleagues were going to have to see her as their leader, not just the chair who manages things for them, and they were going to have to see her in a different light than they had as a peer. One of the things R. C. enjoyed most was the Friday afternoon pitcher with some of her department colleagues at a tavern two blocks from campus. This was an excellent way to unwind after a busy week, and she felt a special kinship with the seven or eight regulars. But these sessions were also ways to let off steam for the participants, usually by bashing the administration or poking fun at other members of the department not in attendance. R. C. realized that as long as she continued to participate in these social events, the regulars would regard her as just one of the group, and the other members of the department would see her as more attached to that group than to themselves. Friday afternoons became the time she had to finish up the work of the week, and she phased out of the tavern group. Every good leader takes advantage of social opportunities for a variety of reasons, but they know that the leader-follower relationship is always present, and the distance between is an arm's length.

In some ways, a person who chooses to be a leader gives up the prerogative of acting and reacting like everyone else (Schein, 1992). J. L. spent a considerable amount of time with his subordinates and always managed to tell them how busy he was, how much he had to

do, and how he was protecting their interests. This did
not have the desired effect of gaining their appreciation.
In fact, the common joke was that J. L. would not be so
busy if he would just stop talking about how busy he
was. The point is, people know intuitively that leaders do
a lot for them, but part of the mystique is for the leader
to appear to do it as if born to it.

Followers want and deserve a leader who is a role
model of their own better natures, not of their lowest ones.
This is an onerous responsibility, especially given the
fact that leaders are, in fact, subject to the same whims
and urges as everyone else. But this is why character,
integrity, honesty, and other such attributes become so
important as leadership qualities. Leaders must have a
code of personal conduct that helps them steer through
the myriad obstacles and temptations life presents. Anyone with power can get others to accomplish any tasks,
and people will do whatever they are compelled to do by
the powers they report to. But people will want to follow only those people in whom they see something of
substance that is better than what they possess. T. R.
is president of a large community college and is widely
recognized as an outstanding community college leader.
Under his leadership the college endowment has grown
many times over, public financial support for the institution has grown exponentially, and business and industry
have stepped forward in unique and innovative partnerships. There is no doubt that the college has prospered
under his leadership. During annual convocations and
other meetings with the employees, T. R. goes over all the
accomplishments and challenges but always drops the
names of the senators, commissioners, governors, and
other people he has associated with on behalf of the college. Unfortunately, the employees see this as indication
of an overly large ego, and rather than feel invigorated
by their shared successes, they feel overworked, under-
appreciated, and disconnected. The difference between

managing and leading is not in the size of the accomplishment. It is the way people feel about what they have accomplished. Excellent leaders do not allow themselves or their behavior to get between the followers and the followers' ownership of the efforts and achievements (Brooks & Brooks, 2005). One cannot argue with the success of T. R.'s management. However, we can wonder what kind of success could be achieved if the followers were impassioned to follow.

There are emotions effective leaders regularly display that are infectious to followers. Among these are empathy, enthusiasm, and passion. Empathy is important, because people want to believe others understand their work and the circumstances of it. Faculty have a basic distrust of administrators who have not taught, for example. Throughout the organization, there are people who believe their jobs are more important than anyone else realizes and that no one understands what they have to go through in order to do them. Leaders cannot possibly know, or have experienced, all the jobs done by all the followers, even in a small work group. They can, however, recognize that everyone has a legitimate reason to feel that he or she is somewhat unique. With this recognition, leaders can communicate to followers that they are, indeed, special with a very important role in the organization.

Enthusiasm and passion are the two attributes that are most captivating to followers. Followers want to know that their leader truly believes in what they are doing and is willing to put the energy into it to make it happen (Brooks & Brooks, 2005). The deadliest words a leader in the organization can say are, "The president says we have to do this." What has to be done will be done, but the leader-follower relationship is compromised. The leader is now a messenger/manager, and the followers are the most minimal resource of human capital, their only value being to be spent. Passion, on the other hand, is fuel. When people feel passion about what they are doing, they move more quickly, smile more, and feel better about coming to work.

J. G. is the owner of one of the last cut-and-sew plants left in the Carolinas. With about 200 employees, he has managed to stay in business by appealing to niches that larger plants, which have all gone south of the border, would not take. Usually this means working with smaller units, such as 300 specialized uniforms rather than several thousand standardized ones. J. G. is passionate about production. When he walks onto the floor, his face literally changes. He cannot contain his smile as he walks among the cutters and sewers and other employees, talking to them, acknowledging their work, and encouraging them. He is not trying to get them to work harder; he is passionate about production, and so are they. He has implemented all the requisite reward systems for manufacturing labor: rewards for exceeding quota, rewards for reduced absences, and recognitions of outstanding performance. But what really drives the employees is their employer's passion for that thing that is larger than individual output: production. They grasp it and enthusiastically pursue it. Wages in this plant are typical for this type of manufacturing, but employee turnover is remarkably low. When J. G. has to hire someone new, he never advertises. He simply tells the employees he has an opening, and he has applicants the following day.

J. G.'s example was presented here because people in academia sometimes come to believe that teaching is the only endeavor within the organization deserving of true passion. Certainly no endeavor deserves it more. But passion, whether intense or mild, is simply a factor of how strongly a person believes in the importance of what he or she is doing. It is existential, in a way, because one endeavor may or may not be more important than another in the overall scope of the organization. How a person chooses to approach his or her work, however, differs greatly. And if that work becomes important to an individual, that individual can approach it with passion. Anyone within an organization who would like to have others follow must truly believe in the importance of what they, together, are trying to accomplish, and that importance will be evident through the leader's enthusiasm and passion.

Informal Leaders Are Neither Born Nor Made—They Are Grown

Most people in an organization are reasonably content to do their jobs and ask nothing more than to be left alone to do them (Kelley, 1992). As long as these people are competent and are of such personality that they do not make coming to work difficult for others, they are very valuable, and they deserve acknowledgment and respect for what they contribute. But colleges and universities have a loftier purpose than most other organizations, and because of this, they attract into their employ people who need to be part of something that is larger than themselves. These people have a basic need to contribute more than the specific skills for which they were hired (Argyris, 1964). Although they might utter the old cliché that everyone is expendable, they have a desire to make a difference in the organization. They know that if they leave today, they will be replaced tomorrow, and students will continue to be taught, grants will be filed, people will get paid, and generally, the work will go on without them. What they would like to believe, however, is that the work will be different and that their special contribution to it will be missed. These are the people within the college or university who basically define its character. They are the ones who lead from where they are (Bennis & Nanus, 1985).

The people who lead from where they are provide the margin between what a college has to be and what it is capable of being. They are followers in that they are following the president, the dean, the department head, or the supervisor. But they are leading in that they are taking those people or processes over which they have authority someplace they would not otherwise go. If it is in the area of financial aid (perhaps the most rule-bound process in the college), the direction might be to increase the number of students who apply or simply to create a physical environment that is friendly and inviting. In purchasing, the direction might be to create communication systems that keep employees updated on their equipment requests. In fact, there is no area of the college that would not be enhanced by the talent and commitment of leadership at that level. People in formal leadership positions at the college need to nurture leadership wherever they see it, not only for what the informal leaders accomplish, but because of the example they set for others.

There is another reason for people in authority to nurture and acknowledge leadership throughout the organization. People who want to do more for the college than just the basics their jobs require of them have bought into the larger purpose of the institution. Whether they can quote the mission statement or not, they believe the work is important; therefore, they have a commitment for it to be successful. These are the people whose influence should be felt throughout the organization. These are the ones who keep the college moving when the formal leaders are not present. Nurtured and encouraged, these informal leaders become the most active followers of the direction set by the formal leaders. In addition, they become opinion leaders, and they have the energy to participate in the committee structure and on the ubiquitous task forces. In other words, they are the ones most likely to become involved in the workings of the college and, as a result, become a tremendous resource of energy, talent, and advice. They might not agree with the president on an issue, but they are committed to the college and, therefore, are open to learning why the president is right, or they are willing to pursue compromise. For all these reasons, informal leaders count, and they have a voice. Formal leaders encourage informal leaders most effectively simply by listening to them.

Good followers take direction well, and good managers know how to direct. But good leaders know that every follower is a potential leader in place who wants to contribute more than just his or her assignment. These potential leaders want to be part of the process. The leaders, on the other hand, have more information and experience than the followers, and they also have a higher stake in the outcome. Therefore, they tend to tell rather than discuss, and they can be impatient waiting for a follower to come to an understanding the leader has already reached. For all these reasons, leaders rush to answers and leap to solutions, rather than allow the followers the opportunity to fully express themselves. The followers, even when they appear to be resisting, are really processing their thinking in order to arrive at the same place as the leader. Blocking this process disconnects the follower from the effort, and rather than being committed to a high-quality outcome, the follower does only what he or she is told. The leader-follower relationship is a partnership (Hollander, 1987; Gardner, 1987). The manager-worker relationship is not.

Conclusion

People in academic institutions are blessed with meaningful work that serves a higher purpose. Yet it is very demanding work, and because it is mission driven, it never ends. There are always more students, another grant, and another semester. The energy, creativity, and passion required for this endless endeavor cannot be sustained by the president alone. Presidents, themselves, have a finite supply of these things. However, presidents, like most other people in the organization, are energized by the palpable hum and buzz of people actively engaged in moving forward and doing things better. When organizations truly value and nurture leadership at all levels, there are few challenges they cannot meet and no better environments in which to work.

References

Argyris, C. (1964). *Integrating the individual and the organization.* New York, NY: John Wiley & Sons.

Bass, B. M. (1985). *Leadership and performance beyond expectations.* New York, NY: The Free Press.

Bennis, W. (1989). *On becoming a leader.* Reading, MA: Addison-Wesley.

Bennis, W., & Nanus, B. (1985). *Leaders: The strategies for taking charge.* New York, NY: Harper & Row.

Brooks, D., & Brooks, L. (2005). *Ten secrets of successful leaders: The strategies, skills, and knowledge leaders at every level need to succeed.* New York, NY: McGraw-Hill.

Etzioni, A. (1961). *A comparative analysis of complex organizations.* New York, NY: The Free Press.

French, J. R. P., & Raven, B. (1959). The bases of social power. In D. Cartwright (Ed.), *Studies in social power.* Ann Arbor, MI: University of Michigan, Institute for Social Research.

Gardner, J. W. (1987). Leaders and followers. *Liberal Education, 73*(2), 4–8.

Hersey, P., & Blanchard, T. (1982). *Management of organizational behavior* (4th ed.). Englewood Cliffs, NJ: Prentice Hall.

Hollander, E. P. (1987). Social psychological perspective on leadership. *Liberal Education, 73*(2), 9–15.

House, R. (1971). A path-goal theory of leader effectiveness. *Administrative Science Quarterly, 16*(3), 321–338.

Kanter, R. M. (1983). *The change masters: Innovation and entrepreneurship in the American corporation.* New York, NY: Simon & Schuster.

Kelley, R. E. (1992). *The power of followership: How to create leaders people want to follow and followers who lead themselves.* New York, NY: Currency Doubleday.

Kouzes, J. M. (1988, January 24). When leadership collides with loyalty. *Forum: The New York Times,* p. 3.

Kuh, G. D., & Whitt, E. J. (1988). *The invisible tapestry: Culture in American colleges and universities* (ASHE-ERIC Higher Education Rep. No. 1). Washington, DC: Association for the Study of Higher Education.

McGregor, D. M. (1960). *The human side of enterprise.* New York, NY: McGraw-Hill.

Ouchi, W. G. (1981). *Theory Z: How American business can meet the Japanese challenge.* Reading, MA: Addison-Wesley.

Pascale, R. T. (1985). The paradox of "corporate culture": Reconciling ourselves to socialization. *California Management Review, 27*(2), 26–41.

Schein, E. H. (1992). *Organizational culture and leadership* (2nd ed.). San Francisco, CA: Jossey-Bass.

Stout, J. K. (1984). The role of self-concept in interpersonal communications. *Supervisory Management, 29*(2), 12–16.

Tierney, W. G. (1988). Organizational culture in higher education: Defining the essentials. *Journal of Higher Education, 59*(1), 2–21.

9

Leadership Is Action: Learning to Lead in Place

Willis M. Watt

Change is inevitable. Schein (1992) indicates that all human systems seek equilibrium. He suggests they seek to maximize their autonomy within their environment. Further he claims coping, growth, and survival involve continuing the viability of the entity in the face of a changing culture and society.

One of the changes occurring in academe during the past several decades involves faculty and administrators. In his 1959 book, *The Idea of a College*, Dr. Elton Trueblood offers a philosophy of what the academic community ought to be like. He warns that "one of the greatest dangers in modern college life is that of an extreme division of labor, especially when it creates too great a distinction between the teaching staff and the administrative staff" (p. 68).

Leadership in the academy has been shifting from a collegial to a business model. Peter Shapiro (2005), senior fellow at the James MacGregor Burns Academy of Leadership, states, "Leadership is an action, not a title, and the ability to lead can be found in every person. Each of us must claim our authority to lead at the right time and in the right place" (p. 1). We find ourselves in an era when we need faculty leadership in the academic community.

As we suggest throughout this book, we need faculty who are willing and able to lead in place. Thus, in this chapter I describe four case studies illustrating what I learned about leading in place. I also offer three general conclusions based on these experiences that reflect what it takes to be an effective leader.

Leadership in the Right Place/Right Time

After graduating in 1980 I accepted a position as an untenured, temporary assistant professor of speech communication at an NCAA Division I land-grant university. At my interview it was repeatedly stressed that this position was for only nine months without any expectation of continuation. The pay was very low considering that I spent the equivalent of 12½ years completing my college education. It was a surprise that I was given a huge office with beautiful antique furniture. However, there was a problem with the office. It was not located in the main building housing the speech communication department. In fact, the office was a considerable distance from the main facility and my department. As a student of organizational communication, I recognized the potential hazard I faced given my isolation from my peers.

I determined that if I was to be successful at this job then I was going to have to do something about my situation. After a couple of weeks on the job I noticed a vacant desk in the main department office. When I inquired about the fact that I never saw anyone at the desk, I was informed that it had been used by a former secretary. The position had not been filled, thus the empty desk. After some thought, I decided to work in my assigned office before my first morning class (usually at 9 a.m.) and then put all my materials I would need for the rest of the day in my briefcase and settled in at the empty desk, making it my unofficial office in the departmental area. By doing this I made myself accessible to administrators, faculty, and students when they came to the departmental office. When the secretaries were on break or were otherwise unavailable, I was there to assist anyone who needed it. I assumed the role of a leader in place. Because I was in the right place at the right time, I made myself accessible.

Eventually, I became indispensable to the department. At the end of my nine-month contract, I was offered the opportunity to teach in both summer sessions (something not normally allowed because of past departmental practice). I was also offered another contract for the next academic year. In essence I had become the unofficial office manager because of my accessible location and taking responsibility to make sure that people's needs were met when they came to the department.

In the fall of my second year at the university, the departmental executive officer (DEO) asked me to chair a search committee for the director of the basic course—a speech communication course all university graduates were required to complete. The committee consisted of three tenured faculty members (two of whom were professors), a tenure-track associate professor, and me (a nontenure-track, temporary assistant professor). The committee identified a candidate who was hired to fill the position. I remained at the university for two more academic years and taught each of the four summers I was there. Before departing to accept a tenure-track position, I was offered a fifth contract. It is my conviction that I was rehired so many times because I made myself available and was willing to accept responsibility beyond what was called for in my job description. When a need existed for someone in the right time and the right place to lead in place, I made sure I was ready and willing to accept the leadership challenge.

So what did I learn about leading in place? (This question reminds me of one of the required journal entries I ask my students in my upper-division communication courses to respond to as they write about their experiences.) It seems obvious to me that Peter Shapiro (2005) is correct: Each one of us must be ready and willing to step up and lead when the time and place are right.

Creating Space for People Not in Formal Authority Positions

In 1984 I interviewed for a debate coach position at an NCAA Division II state university in the central plains. During my interview with the department chair, he made a statement that caught me completely off guard. In a matter-of-fact manner he said, "When you become the chair of the department . . . " To say the least, I was startled. I remember thinking to myself, "Department chair? I just want to get this job!" I did get the offer and accepted the position. Over the next several years I worked long, hard hours to develop a nationally competitive Cross-Examination Debate Association (CEDA) debate program. Then in the spring of 1988, I was called into the chair's office. He asked me if I would be willing to serve as the interim department chair while he was on sabbatical. To me that seemed to be an amazing request, because I was an untenured assistant professor in a department with at least four tenured professors who each had considerable academic administrative experience in addition to many years of service to the university. I took advantage of the opportunity.

During the spring 1989 semester my department chair privately shared the unfortunate news that he had been diagnosed with lung cancer. He asked that I keep the information to myself, which I did. Later that summer, however, I came to the department office to make copies, and my eyes met the gaze of his administrative assistant. A knowing look passed between us as we simultaneously blurted out, "You know about Jim, don't you!" It was a relief to finally be able to share that painful knowledge with another person.

For three years Jim continued to perform his official duties as a professor and an administrator at the university. When it came to his interaction with students, Jim was the epitome of the "professor of the year." He was totally dedicated to them and their learning experience. As might be expected he began to require assistance as his health declined. However, until the very end, Jim remained steadfast in the classroom. In fact, during that final spring semester in 1991, Jim would miraculously arrive at the department parking lot in his faded, powder blue 1965 Volkswagen Beetle. To this day I am not sure how he was able to get from his home to his car and fit his six-foot, six-inch frame into the Beetle to drive to work each day. But he did. When he arrived, his students would wheel his office chair across the parking lot to the door of the Beetle. They would lift Jim and place him in his chair so that he could be rolled to the classroom. Jim would teach his two classes back to back, and then the students would wheel him to his office.

In addition to remaining dedicated to his students, Jim also accomplished his administrative duties. Jim would meet with Kathy, his administrative assistant. He would sign necessary papers and documents and provide her with instructions for the day's work. Shortly thereafter he would ask for me. I would sit with him as he discussed issues such as the interview process of a potential new faculty member, budget and annual reports, and supervision of curriculum and instruction matters. We would brainstorm about what needed to be done and how best to accomplish our mission.

Throughout Jim's three-year battle with cancer, I became more and more responsible for the leadership of the communication department. On top of my regular teaching, scholarly activities, and service to the community, I took on more administrative duties and responsibilities. At one point, as a result of my ever-increasing work involving the duties of the department chair, the academic provost and the college dean met with me to consider an appointment as the interim department chair. After discussing the matter there was unanimous agreement that in the best interest of Jim's emotional, mental, and physical well-being, and his hoped-for recovery from his battle with cancer, it would be better not to make an official move to appoint me as the interim chair. In fact, we determined that I would continue to assist Jim and perform any assigned leadership functions he might send my way. The university community would recognize my signature as authoritative whenever and wherever it might appear in the daily operation of the department. I became unofficially known as the surrogate chair of the communication department. It was in this unofficial leadership role that I learned much about academic leadership.

My mentor, Dr. James I. Costigan, taught me the meaning of courage and dedication. It should be pointed out that the communication department faculty were supportive of this arrangement and worked collaboratively with me to the very end. In spring 1991, one week after the graduation ceremony, Jim lost his battle with lung cancer, but he left a heritage of courage and dedication. His legacy as a professional educator dedicated to teaching students is one that few will ever be able to match.

So what did I learn about leading in place? It seems apparent to me that effective leadership means creating space for people not in formal authority positions. It also seems obvious to me that effective leaders take the time to develop crucial relationships within the academic community. Dr. R. Kirby Godsey, president of Mercer University in Macon, Georgia, affirmed this point in his commencement address to the 2005 graduating class of Campbell University in Buies Creek, North Carolina. He said, "successful leaders . . . develop relationships.

They also listen, take the time to think, and show courage" (Thrasher, 2005, p. B1).

Engaged Leadership

Several years ago I had the opportunity to return to my undergraduate alma mater as the vice president for academic affairs. At that time the NCAA Bible college was seeking initial regional accreditation from the North Central Association of Schools and Colleges (NCA). Because I had some experience working with regional accrediting bodies while working at a state university, the Bible college administration and faculty believed I would be well suited to lead them in this important process. With that knowledge I accepted the position beginning in mid June 1997. A major duty I took on was to serve as the self-study coordinator for the accreditation process. Under the excellent leadership of my predecessor, the initial study and paperwork had been completed.

When I stepped in, it was time to draft the self-study report. It was clear to me that in order to complete this extensive report and submit it to the NCA by mid August, I was going to need a lot of assistance from others at the college. I immediately began to meet with those who would have the background, understanding, and knowledge needed to compile and write the self-study report. I spent a considerable amount of personal and work time gathering information and data as well as doing an analysis of the life of the college and its future. This information processing meant that I had to identify and seek out emergent leadership and not just depend on the designated leadership of the college. Those staff and faculty willing to accept the responsibility of being engaged provided me with very valuable information and insight.

After submitting the self-study report, the next major task was to prepare for the site team's campus visit in October. Having been in the position only a few months, it was critical to give various staff and faculty (and even student leaders) the ability to make autonomous decisions about how we would present ourselves when our visitors arrived on campus. In my formal capacity as vice president for academic affairs, I sought to connect the various activities the staff and faculty were being asked to perform for our common goal (i.e., to be accredited by NCA). Of course, in the midst of all our preparations, in August the college began the academic chore of providing classes and other student services. This meant that many of those who had been stepping up to provide the requisite leadership in place were also having to focus on their primary duties of teaching and providing student services. The good news for me was that I was working with a dedicated cadre who were willing to engage in leadership and go the extra mile for the welfare of the college. I realized that if we were to be successful in achieving our primary goal of accreditation, then I must do my best to set in place support structures that allowed for open and honest communication between me and those I was serving at the college. As Trueblood (1959) suggests, we realized we needed to be a team; that is, we were not just a work group seeking only a common goal, but we held to common values. We also shared a common vision as articulated in our vision statement—to educate, equip, and enrich Christian leaders. Through open and honest communication, we realized that we were more than just a work group with a common goal. We shared a common fate. The success of any one of us impacted the success of the others and the achievement of our goal of regional accreditation. Jointly, we agreed that if we were to achieve our specific goal, and ultimately our vision, we could not be just a working group with a common goal, but we must look for win-win outcomes while listening (not just hearing) to each other. Given our common commitment to the college vision, we sought to be responsible for our actions and collaborate with one another.

Thus, we acted in a manner consistent with the team concept presented by Trueblood.

Teams win and lose as a group, not as individuals. Therefore, we identified what faculty and staff interests were, and I sought to negotiate with them in a collaboration focused on our common goal of regional accreditation. Using this approach I sought to engage them in the leadership process as leaders in place. I pointed out that it was not my self-study report, nor was it my campus visit, it was ours. By the time the visiting team arrived that October, we had held many formal and informal meetings to assess our strengths and weaknesses. In fact, as a result of the collaboration that had been taking place on campus, we had already begun to make a number of changes in the college practice and culture. For example, the library was in need of improvements, so we purchased a significant number of electronic databases and added computer stations. The site visit was a grueling experience, but we came through it with only eight concerns and 21 points of consideration. As just stated, we already had begun to deal with several of the issues even before the site visitation team arrived. Immediately upon receipt of the team's preliminary report, we met to analyze it and to begin working on improving the college experience for our students. An accreditation steering committee was formed, composed of leaders in place from among the staff, faculty, administrators, students, and alumni. It dealt with the issues the site team had shared with us.

Over the next year and a half, we worked hard to remedy the concerns and considerations presented to us. We did not always agree. There was conflict. However, everyone was encouraged to share openly and honestly the matters we were dealing with as we sought to meet the expectations of the NCA. Key leaders were selected and sent to NCA training. We conducted assessments including a strengths-weaknesses–opportunities-threats

(SWOTs) analysis. We held town hall meetings with staff, faculty, students, alumni, and interested external constituencies. In summer 1999 I began to pull together information and data in order to compile and write a second self-study report. We were scheduled to have another site team visit in November 1999 to provide the college with assistance in its preparation for the final site team visit in November 2001 before the NCA decided whether to grant the college's request for initial accreditation.

After the self-study was completed it was my belief that we had successfully addressed the eight concerns and all 21 considerations presented to us by the 1997 site team. I was convinced the college was actually ready for a site team visit for the purpose of making a recommendation for initial accreditation in November 1999. These thoughts were shared with the college's administrative council (president and vice presidents). It was decided to talk with key formal (i.e., department heads and staff) and informal (i.e., those who had been leading in place over the past two and one-half years or longer) leaders to get their input before making a request for a change of status with the NCA. There was consensus to request the status change and ask for consideration for initial accreditation based on the outcome of the November 1999 site team visit. The NCA approved this request and our status was changed. The college began to prepare for the site team's visit. An example of our solid preparation can be seen in the way we internalized our vision statement. The entire academic community understood and supported it.

As part of our assessment of our curricular offerings and in conjunction with our mission statement, the faculty took the reins of leadership and reworked all 22 bachelor degree programs by adding a 10-hour leadership core. The leadership core was not simply a one-size-fits-all component. This required a lot of critical thinking, effort, and time because each 10-hour leadership component was unique to that degree program. Along the way we held many formal and informal meetings. We sought student involvement, and the members of the site team complimented us for the large turnout of students that met with them that November. We strengthened our liaisons with our alumni and external constituencies. As a result of the empowerment process used throughout the accreditation as we engaged in critical examination of who we were and what we wanted to accomplish, the college received a very favorable site team report, and they recommended to the NCA Commission that we be granted a five-year period of initial accreditation. Throughout this period I did my best to instill the belief that we would achieve our reward—NCA accreditation—only if and when everyone took the responsibility to be a leader in the process. As the designated leader in this situation, I made a concerted effort to assist the college personnel in the achievement of their goal by putting into place processes and structures that were clearly defined and supportive of our effort. At the time the college was seeking accreditation, the process normally took four to six years, but because there was an engaged staff and faculty involved in leadership at all levels, we were able to complete the process and receive initial accreditation in two and one-half years.

So what did I learn about leading in place? First, it was apparent to me that if goals are to be met and missions accomplished then engaged leadership is imperative: "Leadership requires stamina, discipline, and hard work" (Godsey as cited in Thrasher, 2005, p. B1). That is to say, we not only need people in all areas of the institution to step up and accept the responsibility to provide leadership, but we also need individuals who have the energy and discipline to do the hard work of leading in place. This is especially true as it applies to those individuals with special skills and knowledge when those items are essential for ensuring success. I also quickly became aware of the reality that the problems of successfully completing the accreditation process were not all that clear, nor were their solutions clearly defined. A leader who wants to establish a leading-in-place culture must recognize that many problems are not clearly defined with easily identifiable answers; therefore, it is necessary to involve others in the search for solutions. Although I had supplied information and written departmental responses to the NCA at a state university, I had not been solely responsible for producing the self-study report. In my situation I had to spend a considerable amount of time learning about the past, present, and projected future of the college. Although I was a graduate of the college (some 20 years or so earlier), I found it necessary to learn about the administration, faculty, staff, and students of the college while learning how to function as a vice president for academic affairs. I was learning who the staff, faculty, and administrators were and what their needs and priorities were personally and professionally. Another part of leading in place was learning how to work with diverse groups (student affairs, admissions, development, academics, and business affairs). This meant I had to learn to collaboratively identify with the various constituent groups the problems and solutions facing their areas of the college in my effort to put together a credible self-study report.

One invaluable leadership skill is communication. Communication is a two-way process of sending and receiving messages to establish mutual understanding (Watt, Crawford, Hashem, Krug, & Turner, 2005). It is not just talking, but also includes listening (receiving). One helpful tactic that was used was the town hall forum. At several levels within the college, leaders stepped onto the platform to facilitate frank and open discussions of the strengths and weaknesses of the college. The town hall meetings were extremely helpful in providing important information used in the completion of the self-study report. Finally, a lot of effort went into the process of seeking regional accreditation. This happened because people felt empowered. They became engaged in making sure the process was successful. Although I compiled and wrote the self-study report, it was clear to me that it was the product of the work of many people leading in place in the service of the college toward our common goal of accreditation.

Doing the Right Thing for the Greater Good

After three years as a full-time academic administrator, I desired to return to classroom teaching on a full-time basis. In 2000 I accepted a position at an NCAA Division III private religious liberal arts college in the South. During the question-and-answer portion of my interview, one of the questions was, what would I do to improve the college's speech curriculum? The college had just completed its latest Southern Association of Colleges and Schools (SACS) accreditation review. An item of concern for the site visitation team was the school's speech program. In my preparation for the interview, I had noted that the curriculum offered by the college was outdated in terms of the offerings generally provided in contemporary speech communication programs. The program reflected the focus of the speech field of the late 1960s and early 1970s. So in response to the question asked by the vice president for academic affairs, I suggested an interdisciplinary major focused on organizational communication and leadership.

When the fall semester began, I quickly took to the joy of full-time teaching. It was a busy semester with a 12-hour teaching load plus an additional 6-hour course overload that I taught in the college's evening program. Not a single person at the college ever formally tasked me with the job of revising the speech curriculum. Yet, recognizing the need, I took responsibility to provide the necessary leadership. A problem existed, so I took the initiative to solve it. On my own, given the curricular needs of the college, I assumed a leading-in-place approach to work on updating the speech communication curriculum. Therefore, I reviewed the speech major and made an initial wholesale makeover of the speech curriculum. This task required networking within the college community. Because it was my first semester at the college, I had to get acquainted with various staff, faculty, and administrators. A major part of my work was building bridges with key personnel across the campus in an effort to involve them in the redesign of the speech program. I talked with key department heads. I also met with faculty in several departments to sell the concept. Although the majority of individuals were extremely supportive of my efforts to improve the speech major, specifically, and the college in general, there was resistance.

As an example of this resistance, the chair of one department did not want me to include any of its courses. His reason was that his faculty already had more students in their classrooms than they could collectively handle. The student-to-teacher ratio at the college at that time was 17 to 1. Including a course (a multisection offering) would likely have only resulted in a minor increase of a student or two in any given section. Over a period of several weeks, I worked with this department chair. Eventually we compromised by deciding to include a course other than the one I felt was the best fit for the proposed major in organizational communication and leadership. What I had sought was a win-win collaboration between our two departments, but that did not take place. Instead, we settled for a lose-lose compromise. Since the course we settled on was not the one that would best serve the students of the college, the students also had to settle for a major program of good, but lower, quality because of the political environment on campus.

Part of the reason we entered this less-than-ideal situation was that the department chair was trying to send a message to the academic dean that his department was understaffed. The department chair saw my request as a way of making a point to the dean. This is why I say it was lose-lose compromise: The ploy was not successful. The academic dean did not increase the department chair's staff. For the time being, the students, completing a viable program, would have to settle for a second-rate course from that particular department.

Not to be discouraged by the outcome of this interaction, I continued to work with other departments. After gaining support from the affected departments, I presented the proposal I had developed to my department. This was a somewhat awkward affair, because after my hire, the speech department had been folded into the English department. At this point, I was confronted with trying to convince a group of interested people of the value of and the necessity for the new major. The speech program (no longer a department) clearly held a stepchild status in the English department. Using what little political capital I possessed, I argued the existing speech major was dated and that SACS expected changes in the program. In addition, I shared that the president and vice president for academic affairs supported the new major. Before the presentation of the new major to the English department, I had reach-tested the idea of the new major with key leaders in the department, including the department chair and other informal leaders. I sensed some benign opposition, but the program was unanimously approved by the department. Later I learned that one of the English faculty members had taught speech at the college and was partially responsible for developing the existing speech major that I was trying to remold and update as a new major in organizational communication and leadership.

Next I had to present the new major to the program planning and evaluation committee. I had to answer questions about personnel, equipment, and spacing needs. The new program received unanimous support at this level of the approval process. Simultaneously, the curriculum committee reviewed the new major. When meeting with the committee, I ran into some slight resistance, which I later attributed to the fact that I had offended the English faculty member by referring to the speech program as outdated. In an academy of slightly more than 100 full-time faculty members, word gets around. Old liaisons and friendships can have a powerful impact on the internal and external environment. Eventually, however, the program was approved. Because the college does not have a faculty senate but operates as a faculty of the whole, it was necessary for me to present the new major before this august group. When I made my final presentation before the whole faculty, I found the vast majority favored the modernized major, but there was a very small group that resisted the proposal. The opposition came from the department that felt it was overworked and understaffed and from a few in my own department who were loyal to their colleague who had helped to develop the original major and had taught those courses in the distant past. A 43-hour interdisciplinary major was approved: It included courses in business, interdisciplinary studies, leadership studies, mass communications, sociology, and speech communication. But the story does not end there. The approved major was a lose-lose compromise for the students. Consequently, over the next year I sought a win-win proposal. By doing the right thing and seeking the greater good of everyone involved, especially the students, I was able to gain approval of a modified 30-hour speech curriculum—an interdisciplinary organizational communication and leadership major with an option for a minor in leadership studies—a win-win for everyone involved.

What did I learn about leading in place? First, this experience underscored the realization that leadership involves taking the initiative to solve problems, but more importantly leading in place means you must sometimes do the right thing and stand by your decision and actions in order to ensure the larger good of the organization. Dr. Godsey was correct when he told the graduates at Campbell University that "leaders are those people who take initiative to solve problems" (as cited in Thrasher, 2005, p. B1). I was also reminded that as a leader seeks to do work, the outcome is more likely to be positive if it can be shown to be in the service of a common goal (e.g., to provide students with a quality learning experience). I learned that if you are going to accomplish a task, it is important to have an academic culture supported by a network that encourages collaboration among people and groups with diverse interests and goals.

I also learned that, like individuals, organizations seek balance. When members of an organization experience tension arising from a perceived imbalance, they will seek to reduce the dissonance. A leader needs to provide a vision of the desired outcome and set it in a reality that others can readily identify with and accept. It should be noted that I initially made a tactical error when proposing the new major to the department. I stated that the current speech major was "outdated, not in step with the times." I failed to value the past. As noted earlier, there were some members of the department who had helped develop the old speech program and had even taught some of the courses in the major. This initial tactical error on my part created unnecessary resistance to my proposal. In fact, the resistance carried over into the deliberations of the curriculum committee and to the faculty as a whole. If the curriculum committee had voted unanimously to adopt the proposed major, then the process would have been complete. Unfortunately, that did not happen. Thus, the proposal had to be presented before the entire faculty and defended there in order to get approval. What I should have done was demonstrate my appreciation for the past while at the same time engendering openness for and acceptance of the new major program.

Conclusions

In this section I share three major conclusions about effective leadership in place: empowerment, collaboration, and encouragement of risk taking. These conclusions are drawn by someone with a 30-year career as a faculty member who has been a department chair, a vice president for academic affairs, and is now a school dean.

Empowerment

The first lesson I learned about leading in place involves empowerment. Empowerment creates a corps of people who can be brought on board to deal with needed change. After we understand who we are and what we hope to accomplish, we must empower others to understand who they are and what they hope to achieve—personally and professionally.

Empowerment frees people to act. Covey (2004), in his book, *The 8th Habit: From Effectiveness to Greatness*, suggests that in order to be a great leader you must "find your voice and inspire others to find theirs" (p. 26). This is the essence of empowerment. It frees people to act. It brings with it a sense of ownership. Tangible results can be achieved, because people are working together as a team with a unified focus. Working with other committed individuals creates a synergistic effect that has the potential to produce extraordinary outcomes (Covey, 1991).

Empowerment should be a part of a leader's repertoire. As we seek to understand and recognize the needs of others, they will be inclined to reciprocate such positive behavior in their dealings with those with whom they are working.

In addition, there is an important ethical dimension of empowerment. While we want to motivate others, it is important to be careful to use persuasion that is not based on authority (especially if you are a designated leader), but on a principle of stewardship recognizing that your position of leadership is held at the will of those working beside you. Essentially what I am saying is that empowered leading in place involves people who are aware of and committed to the needs of others. Such empowered leadership is, therefore, better suited to effective and appropriate communication, thereby benefiting individuals and the organization as a whole.

Collaboration

The second lesson I learned involves the importance of collaboration. An important realization is that, because problems are rarely clearly defined and without easily identified solutions, those who would lead in place must involve others in their efforts. Such leaders need to work together in order to solve problems and achieve organizational goals.

At all levels academic leadership needs to implement collaborative practices. Adopting a collaborative approach means an inclusive rather than exclusive dispersal of information, thereby changing the way problems are solved. Collaboration motivates people to work toward a common vision and goals.

How do we develop and maintain a collaborative work environment? First, involve others in decision-making. Make it clear to them that their opinions are desired and beneficial. Encourage thinking outside the box. By valuing differences of opinion, we create an appreciation for and acceptance of a diversity of viewpoints. This diversity results in the identification of new approaches to meet challenges and take advantage of opportunities.

Successful leadership in place means asking, "What is best for all?" Complex issues are best addressed in a collaborative manner with everyone working together toward the achievement of the organizational vision and its goals. The success of collaboration is enhanced by forming liaisons with other individuals.

Collaboration involves what I call a period of reach-testing, during which we allow all parties to argue and support their own positions. Covey (1991) refers to this as achieving the "3rd Alternative." His third alternative is achieved as a result of collaborative synergy, wherein people "Think Win/Win" (Covey, 1991) and work together to identify what is best for the entire group, not just any one individual or subgroup.

In addition, facilitative-minded leaders recognize the importance of collaboratively involving outside individuals and organizations, which has the potential to bring needed credibility. Individuals and outside organizations can bring important information, data, experience, knowledge, resources, influence, and power to a leader. We should encourage the inclusion of internal and external entities to increase the chance for greater empowerment of others and helping to ensure achievement of the organizational vision and its goals.

In essence, leaders acknowledge through word and deed that leadership exists at all levels of the institution—vertically, horizontally, and laterally. Support of collaboration will facilitate the identification, development, enhancement, and application of effective leadership by those willing to lead in place. Effective leading in place requires the use of collaboration.

Encouragement of Risk Taking

The third and final lesson I learned dealt with the importance of encouraging risk-taking behavior. From time to time, existing power structures and practices must be challenged, because they are neither effective nor efficient. It makes sense then that we develop and promote leadership in place in order to encourage people to take risks to deal with such intolerable conditions.

Sadly, productive change too often cannot be achieved, because people fear failure. Without our encouragement, people are not likely to be willing to take risks. They are unlikely to step up to lead in place. So we must develop an environment where people feel safe.

How does this happen? Leaders must demonstrate to others that taking risks is not only okay, but it is desirable. They should acknowledge that mistakes will be made, but a mistake is not a failure. People need to be confident that you support trial-and-error learning. When our interactions reflect such an environment, the result will be a sense of trust. Then people will trust you and your leadership.

Without risk takers the status quo is likely to roll along unhindered, much to the joy of some people in the organization. Tichy and DeVanna (as cited in Northouse, 2004) encourage "dissent" and allowing people to "disagree" (p. 182). This means that from time to time we must support those willing to break down old structures and practices while putting new ones in their places. Encouraging risk taking means allowing risk taking—to ensure necessary change to achieve organizational success—even the occasional mistake.

Because traditional approaches intended to handle change too often do not work or, in fact, have failed, we need to identify and work with those who are not satisfied with the current state of affairs. As we encourage risk taking, it is important that we clearly communicate with people and motivate them to accept the idea that their activities should serve the academic community, not just themselves or some pet project they are working on, to the detriment of the overall community. We must gain their commitment to the general welfare of all persons and the organization.

Summary

In this chapter I shared four case studies involving leadership and what I learned about leadership. I also discussed three general areas concerning what it takes to be an effective leader in place—at the "right time and in the right place" (Shapiro, 2005, p. 1).

When the call for volunteers goes out, we need people to step forward. Alexander and Helen Astin, of the UCLA Higher Education Research Institute, claim it is possible for any individual to be a leader and to make a difference (as cited in Crawford, Brungardt, & Maughan, 2000). Accepting their claim, I believe we should promote leading in place. Everyone should be given the opportunity to accept the responsibility to lead. When we empower individuals, use collaboration, and let people take risks, then we give others what it takes to lead effectively. Leading in place offers people access to a leadership paradigm designed for the betterment of the academy.

Author Note

This chapter is dedicated to Dr. James I. Costigan, friend and mentor.

References

Covey, S. R. (1991). *Principle-centered leadership.* New York, NY: Summit.

Covey, S. R. (2004). *The 8th habit: From effectiveness to greatness.* New York, NY: The Free Press.

Crawford, C. B., Brungardt, C. L., & Maughan, M. (2000). *Understanding leadership: Theories and concepts.* Longmont, CO: Rocky Mountain Press.

Northouse, P. G. (2004). *Leadership: Theory and practice* (3rd ed.). Thousand Oaks, CA: Sage.

Schein, E. H. (1992). *Organizational culture and leadership* (2nd ed.). San Francisco, CA: Jossey-Bass.

Shapiro, P. (2005). Too many leaders? . . . or do we use the term "leader" too freely? *News & Tools Leadership, 1*(2), 1–2.

Thrasher, A. (2005, May 10). A class of young and old. *The Fayetteville Observer*, pp. B1, B6.

Trueblood, E. (1959). *The idea of a college.* New York, NY: Harper & Brothers.

Watt, W. M., Crawford, C. B., Hashem, M., Krug, E. L., & Turner, J. D. (2005). *Speech communication: Theories and practices* (3rd ed.). Boston, MA: McGraw-Hill.

10

Leadership as Place

Ellen Russell Beatty, Robert Page

Institutions of higher learning are subject to powerful constituencies and contextual factors that can undermine effective implementation of strategic initiatives. In the academic environment, place and context may be as important as content for successful leadership. This is particularly true at the present time, because institutions of higher learning face challenges on a variety of fronts. This places unprecedented pressure on administration and faculty to redefine the way postsecondary education is organized and delivered. Organizations such as the Carnegie Foundation and the Association of American Colleges and Universities (AAC&U; 2002) have identified broad reforms to address these concerns effectively. Given these new demands that may make the lives of students, faculty, and administrators more challenging, securing commitment from these stakeholders is hardly assured. Management research suggests the need for effective leadership to guide implementation of these new strategic initiatives. In this chapter we explore how some of the conventional wisdom concerning effective leadership in the private sector does not apply well to higher education, where exciting visions, compelling strategies, and elegant action planning do not ensure success. Instead, effectiveness often rests on a *mastery of place* and on the contextual issues that seem to underlie and shape effective leadership. Excellent technique without contextual mastery is necessary but not sufficient. In this chapter we review academic leadership theory and present our analysis of leadership effectiveness, illustrated with Dr. Beatty's experiences as academic vice president.

Environmental Trends in the Academy

Higher education has moved into a new millennium in which a college degree has become the rule instead of the exception, unlike any other time in history. This is the inevitable result of a shift away from an industrial and goods-based society towards a knowledge- and service-based society (AAC&U, 2002; Finkelstein, 2003; Rowley & Sherman, 2001), where the best jobs require higher education. Consequently, students and their communities tend to regard a college degree as a prerequisite professional credential for a successful career and a good life (Barker, 2000; Clowes, 1996; AAC&U, 2002). Ironically, it is this very success in becoming legitimized as an institutionalized norm of American society that lies at the root of higher education's most pressing challenges.

Finkelstein (2003) argues that when public education offers universal access, it becomes increasingly central to government institutions—in terms of the importance of the service being offered and the proportion of the budget required to provide the service. In short, higher education in the public sector has evolved into the status of a quasi-public utility, and some argue it should be managed and evaluated as such, using the principles of cost control, accountability, and efficiency that the business world applies to utilities. Although others dispute the functionality of applying a business model to organizations dedicated to developing the mind, intellect, and character of their students, the public is suspicious (Clowes, 1997; Elfin, 2003; Finkelstein, 2003; Reardon & Ramaley, 1996). Critics allege that higher education is organized—from classroom architecture to graduation standards—around the university and faculty interests and does not serve the learning needs of students, particularly nontraditional students (i.e., older students, part-time students, transfer students, etc.), very well (Fuhrmann, 1997; Rowley & Sherman, 2001; Smith, 2004). Universities are being asked to provide evidence to back their claims that they deliver quality student learning outcomes, and many are finding this process extremely difficult.

Universities must cope with the following trends:

- *Increasing competition.* Traditional comprehensive and liberal arts institutions are being effectively challenged by a variety of nontraditional alternatives, ranging from specialty and virtual colleges to company and corporate institutions such as the University of Phoenix (Rowley & Sherman, 2001).
- *Resource constraints.* Since the mid 1990s, average costs have increased 50%, but public spending in higher education has dropped 12%, and the competition for private funding has dramatically increased. These trends are unlikely to reverse themselves in the near future (Carnevale & Strohl, 2001; O'Meara, Kaufman, & Kuntz, 2003; Rowley & Sherman, 2001).
- *Nontraditional students.* Traditional students who enter college full-time shortly after completing high school now account for less than half of a typical student body. Nontraditional (i.e., older, part-time, transfer, at-risk, etc.) students have different learning styles and support needs and may not be serviced well (AAC&U, 2002; Rowley & Sherman, 2001).
- *Accountability.* Although higher education is increasingly expensive, it has not justified its existence.

Quality standards and evidence of student learning outcomes are inconsistent and not encouraging. Demands for the systematic measurement and documentation of higher education's value added are growing (Massy, 2003; Smith, 2004).

- *Learning outcomes.* A wide range of new educational strategies to improve student learning outcomes have been proposed, including learning communities, interdisciplinary courses or modules, sequenced curricular clusters, and new delivery media, making the educational process more comprehensive and complex than ever before (AAC&U, 2002; Smith, 2004).

- *Technology.* Faculty face an explosion of technology applications for teaching, research, and communications. New technologies bring challenges to an evolving pedagogy, demanding enhanced communications and information transfer expectations. In addition, technology redefines availability and accessibility and catalyzes changing research practices (O'Meara, Kaufman, & Kuntz, 2003).

At the center of this environment of change is the academic vice president. Although the array of legitimate initiatives is virtually endless and their rationales compelling, most of these require increased resource support, and that is not forthcoming (Carnevale & Strohl, 2001; Rowley & Sherman, 2001). In fact, there seems to be an almost inverse relationship in operation: The intensity of the demands for documented quality and increased accountability often match a corresponding decline in available resources at state universities (Beatty, Page, & Bermudez, 2004). This emerging situation leaves leaders in higher education caught between a rock and a hard place—delivering increasingly complex services with empirically verifiable effective student learning outcomes in an era of diminished resource support (Massy, 2003). The question becomes, how can academic leaders inspire their professors and staff to do more with less?

Excellence is no longer an option—it is a competitive necessity. Faculty energies are consumed by greater research demands than ever before. Student energies are diverted to work and family responsibilities as never before. Administrative energies focus on opportunistically securing dwindling resources as never before. And yet, without mutual cooperation, the long-term viability of institutions of higher education is problematic.

When Beatty first entered academic administration eight years ago, these challenges loomed large. Originally a teacher's prep normal school, her college had become a comprehensive, level II master's institution—a full state university. Meeting the standards set by the National Council for Accreditation of Teacher Education seemed only a distant hope. Faculty members were overloaded with 12-credit teaching loads, advising responsibilities, university service commitments, increasingly underprepared students, and increasing demands for research and scholarly contributions within their professorial roles. Administrators faced declining resources and increasing demands for accountability (e.g., accreditation standards, assessment initiatives, and legislative demands). Students faced spiraling enrollment costs, decreased availability of scholarships and grants, and increasingly difficult class scheduling. Further, mutual trust and understanding among everyone involved was at an all-time low.

Responding to public concerns and competitive influences, the state legislature, the Board of Trustees, and the university system office maintained that excellence is no longer an option but rather a competitive necessity. However, different constituencies have varied opinions about what excellence is. Faculty tend to define excellence in terms of research output more than ever before. Students are redefining the nature of undergraduate education away from an intensive four-year experience into a longer, multiyear odyssey, during which studies compete with work and family responsibilities for their energy and attention. Administrators focus whatever activities are necessary to secure external resources, which are dwindling in the private and public sectors. Despite these competing interests, without mutual cooperation, the long-term viability of many institutions of higher education becomes problematic (Rowley & Sherman, 2001). Administrators like Beatty are expected to take initiative and successfully resolve these complexities through effective leadership.

Enter Effective Leadership

Effective leadership can be defined as leadership that influences followers to broaden their understanding, elevate their goals, increase their confidence, and perform beyond normal expectations (Avolio & Yammarino, 2002; Dvir, Eden, Avolio, & Shamir, 2002; Shin & Zhou, 2003). Effective leadership builds on the human need for meaning by linking it with institutional purpose. Effective leadership is often manifested through the following dimensions:

- *Consideration.* Leaders develop a relationship of trust and respect with their employees. They solicit, welcome, and act on employee feedback as part of their commitment to continuously improve things. Employees are encouraged to challenge the status quo, exercise their creativity, become involved in change initiatives, and feel ownership for the innovations which result (Burns, 2003; Shin & Zhou, 2003).
- *Leadership communication.* The vision is consistently reinforced by a leadership communication style that shares information openly and candidly throughout the organization in terminology that employees can

understand and relate to (Avolio & Yammarino, 2002; Galford & Drapeau, 2002). In their assessments, the most effective leaders tend to be brutally realistic about current problems but endlessly upbeat about future possibilities (Collins, 2001).

- *Compelling goals and vision.* Followers are energized by articulated, mutually beneficial goals and priorities that give employees an exciting "big picture" of the future of the organization and their place in it (Avolio & Yammarino, 2002; Collins, 2001; Galford & Drapeau, 2002; Shin & Zhou, 2003).

- *Alignment.* Effective leaders align key elements of their organizations to support their vision of change (Cummings & Worley, 2001). Peters and Waterman (1982) popularized the concept of organizational alignment with the McKensie 7–8 framework, which was later applied to higher education (Rowley & Sherman, 2001). This model suggests that organizational effectiveness demands a balance among strategy, structure, systems, shared values, skills, staff, and style.

Private sector leaders align their organizations to accomplish strategic objectives primarily through two strategies: restructuring organizational systems and recruiting proactive staff (Collins, 2001; Galford & Drapeau, 2002; Rowley & Sherman, 2001). Most importantly, leaders must select and retain the right people with the right attitudes and the right abilities. They need skilled workers committed to achieving excellence primarily through implementing the strategic vision of the organization and overcoming any obstacles they encounter—whatever it takes. They also need to identify and prune out obstructionists who are pursuing obsolete or opportunistic agendas that undermine the new strategic initiatives (Collins, 2001; Galford & Drapeau, 2002).

The prospect of being an effective leader in higher education is a daunting one because of problematic alignment. Most leaders do not have unilateral control over strategy, structure, or staff. Instead, academic governance involves careful integration of trustees, collegial governance (bodies usually involving both faculty and students), and administrative governance (Rowley & Sherman, 2001; Shinn, 2004). In the case of public education, powerful union constituencies such as the American Association of University Professors (AAUP) and the American Federation of Teachers (AFT) may be involved as well. In such a higher education environment, the following prerequisites for alignment between strategy, structure, and staff become problematic:

- Selecting recruits who, beyond their discipline, support university goals
- Restructuring academic units to support strategic goals
- Convincing critics to give new initiatives a chance
- Replacing stifling bureaucratic controls with enabling cultural controls
- Reaching consensus on any major decision
- Designing compensation systems to reward strategic activities
- Systematically budgeting resources to support strategic initiatives

Given the limitations on legitimate authority and the presence of powerful competing constituencies, effective leadership is truly a multistakeholder balancing act. Accomplishing this requires all four of the leadership dimensions mentioned earlier, each of which is further explored here.

Consideration

The underlying governance assumptions at most universities reflect liberal arts values in that all important policies will be formulated through a shared governance process. In this idealized shared governance process, the faculty have as much decision-making power as the administration, all college faculty are eligible to partici- pate, and faculty as a whole meet to make important curricular and policy decisions (Shinn, 2004). The entire notion of the academic community rests on principles of collegiality and involvement, and the success or failure of strategic planning initiatives often rests on the degree of faculty participation in the decision-making process. With participation comes ownership, enthusiasm, com- mitment, and a greater chance that decisions "accurately reflect the administrative and academic realities of the campus" (Rowley & Sherman, 2001, p. 178).

At the same time, the greater the participation, the more unwieldy, time-consuming, and contentious the process becomes. Inclusivity brings those who would undermine or subvert the initiative to suit their own opportunistic agendas to the same table along with those who would support and advance it. Committees primar- ily designed to create the illusion of consent by having all parties at the table run significant risks of, at best, slowing decision processes down and, at worst, produc- ing bad decisions or paralyzing the process altogether (Ewell, 2004; Moore, 2003; Parker, 1998; Rowley & Sher- man, 2001). Parker concludes that formal representative structures are not always collaborative and that success- ful collaborative groups are not always representative.

Some researchers suggest that positive mental atti- tude is critical in selecting members for task forces and committees wrestling with issues of strategic focus and vision. Members do not need to agree on what changes need to take place, only on the notion that change is necessary and that a broad range of innovations should be considered (Moore, 2003). Functional selection pro- cesses demand awareness. Effective leaders remain in touch with what is actually going on in their institu- tions. This requires a deep knowledge of group history, an understanding of intergroup dynamics, a systemic relationship, and a commitment to fairness and balance. On the basis of this reputation, while individual actors may disagree with the outcomes, they can respect the process.

Beyond group dynamics, individual relationships are critical. Although individuals may be concerned about the short-term implications of leadership decisions, an ongoing coaching and mentoring relationship reassures them of meaningful long-term development and benefit. Trust requires their appreciation of a long-term investment in their personal interests and agendas. People need reassurance that they will meaningfully develop because of the institution, instead of in spite of it.

An example of consideration in place. When the university decided to rework the strategic plan, Beatty noted that the planning of the initial effort included only nominal faculty participation. Academic affairs reached out to the faculty senate to invite more faculty feedback and involvement. The Faculty Academic Strategic Planning (FASP) committee was formed with representatives from all the major schools on campus. This put teeth into the administrative reassurance that academic considerations would be given top priority. The proposal was met with considerable enthusiasm. The FASP committee members met every week for more than a year, made substantive contributions, and continued to assist the administration in the meaningful development and implementation of academic strategic policy.

This philosophy follows the general approach of *mutual simultaneous interaction* (MSI). This approach is built on the principle of mutual trust and reciprocity. The faculty's feedback gave Beatty greater leverage to influence evolving strategic planning, and her action reassured them that their opinions and suggestions were being taken seriously. This positive self-fulfilling prophecy creates a mutually reinforcing amplification loop (Weick, 1979).

Communication

Consideration is either systematically reinforced or undermined by subsequent communication patterns. Open dialogue and candor do wonders for the mutual trust and respect that underlie consideration, but there are other options. In the academy, or virtually any bureaucratic organizational context, office politics and power games tend to use information and communication as a weapon. Withholding information is a classic power tactic, and systematically distorting or spinning communication is a classic political maneuver (Mintzberg, 1983; Pfeffer, 1972). Both are relatively toxic to developing and maintaining any sense of alignment and effectiveness in the university.

Leadership communication has long been recognized as a critical factor in organizational effectiveness. In the university context, however, merely modeling open and candid communication, while valuable, is not enough. In an environment where powerful constituencies with competing interests are constantly being tempted to turn communication into an opportunistic weapon, leaders must insist on the free and open sharing of authentic communication and accurate information from everyone involved. We are not sure whether discerning relative truth from distortion results from leadership analysis, instinct, gut feel, or some combination of these, but leaders who have that ability are invaluable. Maintaining positive communication requires aggressive confirmation of dubious "facts" offered up in argument and the immediate confrontation of potential character assassination. Beatty carries this principle to its logical conclusion. She has been known, on occasion, to respond to vicious accusations by picking up the phone in the middle of the conversation and calling the person accused for more real-time feedback.

An example of communication in place. Beatty recalls a satisfying and successful experience transpiring as a consequence of a deliberative approach to working with the academic deans at her institution. When Beatty began working with them, they had neither a collective view nor a shared sense of community. An internal focus on effectively running their different schools had naturally resulted in somewhat of a "silo" or "chimney" mentality (Cummings & Worley, 2001). Further, these deans valued leadership activities but felt trapped by the tyranny of seemingly endless, urgent administrative duties. They voiced their frustration concerning their academic roles by describing their positions as ones with high responsibility and little power. Indeed, one academic dean lamented that the role had deteriorated to a "bureaucratic manager with paper-pushing authority."

To remedy this problem, Beatty based her approach on personal experience and on the philosophy of Robert G. Kraft (2000) with a focused and sustained effort toward enhancing the work of the deans. She designed a series of sessions that emphasized intuitive, relational, inclusive, spontaneous, impassioned, and communal values. An important goal was to facilitate the usual business meetings in a manner that encouraged an exploration of issues from a collective viewpoint based on a shared sense of community.

She set the context by arranging for refreshments at each and every meeting, because it is much harder to be negative while eating good food. She sent out inspirational thoughts and shared inspiring, positive reading material before each meeting, and she held a brief discussion of interesting issues, much like a graduate seminar. The meeting room changed from a former women's dormitory to the posh boardroom in the library. Other strategies included regular weekly meetings as a group, concentrated agendas supported with pertinent documents, follow-up assignments, allotment of ample time to discuss important issues candidly, interaction with invited guests from all units of the university, rotation of accountability for reporting and communicating, and an explicit emphasis on confidentiality and respect.

The primary motive was to improve communication between and among the educational leaders of the university. There was a need to capitalize on the talents of this able and willing cohort. Beatty used Chickering and Gamson's (2001) "Applying the Seven Principles for Good Practice in Undergraduate Education," including team-building efforts with the deans: encouraging frequent contact, developing reciprocity and cooperation, encouraging active learning, giving prompt feedback, emphasizing time on task, communicating high expectations, and respecting diverse talents.

The deans now function as a collaborative cohort, which previously had been a stated goal but not an operational reality. They have become quite adept at doing what is best for the institution rather than just for their individual units. The feedback has been unanimous in expressing an appreciation of this change in thinking from school/unit advocacy to a sense of institutional responsibility. The deans heretofore were handicapped by a lack of understanding and knowledge about how the university functions. They have become actively engaged in strategic planning and implementation and are truly moving the organization toward excellence.

The deans confronted intriguing but important problems and often grappled with ideas, which forced them to reexamine their assumptions—particularly concerning resource allocation. It took courage to be reflective about problems within their respective units and the university; however, the deans acted with mutual respect for one another. This deliberate focus on taking stock fostered learning and growth among the individuals directly responsible for student, faculty, and programmatic success. Through these planned sessions based on informed and candid dialogue, the propensity to lay blame on a larger and vague institution was discarded. Instead, the group developed a strong sense of shared commitment to success. An unintended consequence was a keen appreciation for and loyalty to Beatty's role and responsibilities due to the development of a shared sense of governance. She was successful in making each person feel an important part of the academic affairs enterprise rather than a manager of a particular unit.

She used this same philosophy and strategic approach with the Office of Management and Institutional Research (OMIR). Long-standing problems within the university in the collection, analysis, interpretation, storage, and dissemination of information significantly impeded the institution's ability to utilize data-based decision making. The implementation of the OMIR model changed the supervisory and reporting structure, corrected inefficient communication, and improved accountability. For the first time, we now have accurate workload data per the collective bargaining agreement contract achieved through this thoughtful, collaborative, and time-consuming process. The improved results are evidenced by accurate and accessible data for unit leaders. In addition, these outcomes have improved the morale of the individuals involved in institutional research, since they have experienced an enhanced sense of mastery. The ability to deliver needed services in a timely and effective manner has revitalized the personnel within the unit.

These successful efforts with the deans and OMIR have been good for the institution as a whole. By using sound principles of teaching and learning coupled with an emphasis on important values, Beatty was able to mobilize change through effective leadership. The results have engendered a sense of pride and satisfaction in all participants.

Compelling Vision/Goals

With a foundation of consideration and communication, "vision" becomes more than a buzzword. Visions can be defined as vivid, compelling concepts that capture the motivation and commitment of those who accept them (Pence, 2003). Shared vision involves:

> creating a sense of purpose that binds people together and propels them to fulfill their deepest aspirations. Catalyzing people's aspirations doesn't happen by accident; it requires time, care and strategy. Thus the discipline of building vision is centered around a never-ending process, whereby people in an organization articulate their common stories—around vision, purpose, values, why their work matters, and how it fits into the larger world. . . . Visions which tap into an organization's deeper sense of purpose, and articulate specific goals that represent making that purpose real, have unique power to engender aspiration and commitment. (Senge, Kleiner, Roberts, Ross, & Smith, 1994, pp. 298–299)

Without the clarifying and unifying effects of a vivid and compelling vision, opportunism and turf wars often result in office politics and anarchy (Pence, 2003).

Business leaders have the added advantage of being able to terminate obstructionists who do not share that vision and to recruit new players with an explicit selection criterion of buying into that vision (Collins, 2001). This creates an ideological congruence that offers great advantages:

> To mold the minds of individuals according to a definite pattern creates a homogeneous organization, and this is an enormous aid to communication. A broad context of understood meanings ensures that in the performance of assigned tasks the spirit as well as the letter will be observed. Similarly, emotional identification with the orga-

nization creates resources of energy that may increase day to day effort and, especially, be summoned in times of crisis or threat. (Selznick, 1957, p. 18)

Academic leaders have much less control over selection and, particularly in union environments featuring a tenure system, very little say over long-term retention and termination (other than for cause). Unable to build ideological consensus through selection and retention decisions, educational leaders must influence constituencies with a variety of value systems and agendas to accept this vision. Given the lack of ideological homogeneity, they never completely succeed—gaining consensus on any vision of major change is virtually impossible (Rowley & Sherman, 2001; Stimpert, 2004). Further, because part of the fundamental mission of academia is to explore, if not nurture, a variety of creative ways of thinking about a wide variety of subject matter, ideological congruence may be a dysfunctional goal in the first place.

In such an environment, any articulation of a vision empowers opponents as well as supporters, giving them the specifics they need to begin to resist or openly attack the change initiative. Explicitly stated goals—especially on complex issues—serve as focal points around which a previously fragmented and fractious opposition can organize (Dixit & Nalebuff, 1991; Quinn, 1977). More seriously, when the future is turbulent and uncertain, settling on a specific vision may be premature. In the words of a chief executive, "The future can make fools of us all" (Quinn, 1977, p. 24). Once a top leader publicly announces a goal, it can become very difficult to change. Changing the goal broadcasts that the leader was in error and that all those pursuing the goal were on the wrong track. Such conclusions create political vulnerabilities that, if exploited by the opposition, can have disastrous results (Rowley & Sherman, 2001). Consequently both

the executive's ego and those of the people in supporting programs become identified with the goal, creating
a strategic trap known as "escalation of commitment."
Consequently, leaders must be careful with visions,
understanding that "goal announcements centralize the
organization. Such statements tell subordinates that
certain issues are closed and that their thoughts about
alternatives are irrelevant" (Quinn, 1977, p. 22).

To avoid that trap, leaders should not develop visions
to impart to their followers; instead, they encourage their
followers to take initiative and develop visions to share
with their leaders. In this sense, they are more like gar-
deners, providing the support, encouragement, and
guidance for broad-based strategic thinking and then
thinning and pruning out whatever grows to focus on
the most promising initiatives (Wilkins, 1990). Beyond
encouraging innovation and initiative, such strategies
manage risks well by deflecting blame (Dixit & Nalebuff,
1991). The gardening metaphor is particularly appropriate for higher education, given the resource constraints
that inevitably make successful implementation difficult. In such a context, having a credible vision is not
enough—it is the discretionary effort and perseverance
of the actors that determine whether the initiative sur-
vives (Zolner, 2003).

A compelling example of vision in place. Researchers
in higher education warn that introducing any vision
linked with fundamental changes raises resentment and
creates intense opposition (Rowley & Sherman, 2001).
Unfortunately, Beatty did not take Rowley and Sherman
to heart before she launched on a problematic and very
challenging vision strategy. Beatty noted that if she were
to summarize her experiences with vision, they would be
titled "Worshipping on the Altar of Vision: Or, Oh What a
Mistake!" In one particular school, the enrollments had
plummeted over the course of a few years. The faculty
were taken somewhat by surprise, because the pipeline

of ample numbers of students had been rather suddenly affected by external forces. A changing regional economy, rising tuition, and reduced employee tuition reimbursement made for a considerable downturn. The prevailing wisdom at the time was that resources were directly tied to enrollment numbers. Consequently, the faculty within the school voted to substantially lower the grade point average and essentially embrace a de facto open admissions policy. The unintended consequences of this seemingly artful maneuver were to lower standards within the major and to undermine the reputation of the school. Underprepared students did not have access to the mentoring and advisement they needed to compensate for their ability gaps. A disincentive for faculty to invest in sound guidance and advising developed because of rapidly escalating numbers of majors in need of counsel. Too many reports of underprepared graduates from this school were filtering back to the university.

Within the university, students looking for the path of least resistance found haven in some of these programs. Why concern oneself with grades in prerequisite course work when the declaration of major became synonymous with admission to the program? Word spread and students within the university who ordinarily might not seek application now sought entrance. The change in standards did not attract students from outside the university as originally thought. The original intention was to implement this strategy as a temporary measure and return to the original admission and progression standards when enrollments improved. During this extended interval, faculty morale within the school decreased, and the frustration level rose. The university began to experience this school as one in which quality had decidedly slipped.

Beatty's resolve was to assist this group of faculty to envision programs of improved quality and to work collaboratively toward this goal. Given such clear negative feedback from important external constituencies, she assumed the faculty were experiencing a high felt need for change and would welcome the improvements. Instead, her efforts were met with opposition and resistance from some quarters. This reaction initially took her by surprise. How could they not support a vision as virtuous as motherhood and apple pie? What possible basis could there be for a negative reaction to a better program? To her astonishment, some of the faculty were acting similarly to proverbial adolescents, stepping backwards toward the precipice. Were they oblivious to the consequences? The fact remained that they did not experience their plight with the same sense of being on the brink as she did.

The university administration shares the blame for this failure. Over the years, a series of ineffective deans had created a fundamental cynicism and inward focus among some of the faculty that proved unexpectedly difficult to change. Beatty assumed that a promising improvement plan, on the basis of its rational merits, would be quickly accepted by a faculty whose training and research focused on the rational analysis of complex problems with the goal of maximizing positive outcomes and minimizing negative consequences. Until she dealt with the emotional legacy of mistrust, cynicism, feelings of betrayal, and fears for self-preservation, rational merits were rendered powerless, and subject to the rationalizations du jour. In this case, context had become a trap some faculty had willingly fallen into and seemed reluctant to abandon. As the adage states, "better the evil you know."

Beatty's prematurely enacted vision roused a sleeping giant of antagonism because of a variety of reasons. Some faculty felt burned out after former administrators asked them for extensive service and planning activities that proved to be relatively fruitless, and resented a potentially increased work load. Some fell victim to

learned helplessness, fearing that whatever one temporary administrator put in place could easily be undone by
the next administrator, making Beatty's initiatives little
more than a "flavor of the month." Others noticed that
since "nice guys" tended to be ignored, their only chance
for change was to act out. Others were more opportunistic, realizing that some changes might result in a cut-
back of personal revenue–generating activities such as
consulting or lucrative summer course offerings.

As she reflected on the situation, Beatty realized that
she had tread on the sacred ground of faculty autonomy
because of her certainty about a vision for excellence.
Years of distrust concerning diminishing resources
and unilateral decisions caused some to choose poorly.
Beatty's timing for vision implementation was not in
sync with the faculty. Their tolerance for ambiguity was
depleted. In some contexts, the single-minded and persistent pursuit of worthy goals is ineffective. We are not
sure whether this was a case of too little, too late, or
too much, too late, but in either case, until the context
improved, the vision would not take hold.

This school followed a risky reactive gambit called
"brinkmanship" (Dixit & Nalebuff, 1991). From this perspective change is futile until there is sufficient perceived need for change shared among most key players.
Although leaders can allow this perceived need to build
naturally in response to environmental trends and pres-
sures, the process can be deliberately accelerated. By
allowing certain internal problems to escalate into public crises through calculated inaction, restricted communication, and office politics, leaders gain the leverage
they need to demand more fundamental reforms. This
proven strategy flies in the face of most effective leadership models, which call for a clear vision exemplified
by a committed and persistent leader. This is the lifeguard metaphor—in an open-water rescue, if the victim
is flailing around and tries to drown the lifeguard upon

approach, just wait at a safe distance. All of that energy cannot be maintained, and victims will be much easier to rescue when they are exhausted.

Perhaps such clarity is only enabled by a sufficient and profound experience of chaos. Beatty has reconsidered what might have been done with the school. They should have experienced the full consequences of their self-made crisis. She considered them to be on the brink, facing public exposure of the decline in quality. Her genuine concern for the reputation of the university led her to move too fast to protect the larger institution. In this case, many faculty were more attuned to their fears than to the opportunities that were presented to them, and for a short while Beatty did not fully appreciate this degree of misalignment (Rowley & Sherman, 2001).

Alignment

Curricular reforms outlined by organizations such as the Carnegie Foundation and AAC&U have the potential to restore alignment between environmental demands (from students, parents, accreditation agencies, legislatures, etc.) and strategic planning in higher education. However, successful implementation of these new strategies must overcome powerful misalignments within the organization.

For example, public state institutions are often trapped by the *marginalization paradox* (Beatty, Page, & Bermudez, 2004):

- Nontraditional students require more expensive support to succeed.
- Students with the greatest resource needs tend go to institutions receiving lower resource allocation (state universities and community colleges).
- Inadequate resource support contributes to poor learning outcomes.

- Poor learning outcomes lead to resource allocation cuts.
- Resource allocation cuts make maintaining or gaining accreditation difficult.
- To increase revenues, admissions of nontraditional students increase.
- As class loads increase and resources decline, teaching quality suffers and resistance to workload increases for documentation and assessment.
- With problematic documentation of student learning outcomes, legislators push for further cuts in resource allocation.

An example of alignment in place. An example of this marginalization paradox struck home with significant impact for our institution in 2004. The Board of Trustees, in consultation with the system office, mandated an English and Mathematics proficiency requirement, affecting all students in the public higher education system in the state. This seems an illustration of being in agreement on core values, specifically that all students should read, write, and calculate at a college level as a prerequisite to progression through the university system. We were in perfect alignment on core values and completely in misalignment regarding resources and structure. The faculty senate was rightfully outraged, because the underpreparedness of students had been a critical complaint for a number of years. The faculty position was that students were increasingly not prepared for college-level performance and that resources were lacking to resolve this in any way. The mandate from the board seemed a grievous assault representing the inability to understand faculty concerns. Indeed, the mandate to impose an external prohibition without any additional resources outraged the faculty. They felt as if the board enacted a blame-the-victim mandate without consultation with the faculty.

Notice that the proficiency requirement itself was not the target. In fact, many faculty longed for these kinds of goals. The problem was that the requirement was regarded as unachievable and unrealistic in the current university context. This was a classic example of a "No Child Left Behind" mandate without any resources. Because declining resources undermine curricular efforts, maintaining quality becomes increasingly difficult but nonetheless critical for proving legitimacy in the eyes of a demanding legislature and public. The faculty considered this to be assessment in its worst form by an external body both ignorant and uncaring about the driving forces leading to the predicament. The faculty was insulted by this negative attribution of poor quality in public higher education, particularly by outsiders who were responsible for diminishing resources. Beatty's role was to engage the faculty in investing in the new proficiency mandate in their own best interest. It was difficult to overcome the desire to form an alliance with the faculty against the wishes of the board. Despite her agreement with the underlying goal of improved student performance and mastery, Beatty was concerned about the paradox of an access mission accompanied by a mandate to demand high student performance. How would we be able to sustain quality without compromising our mission and jeopardizing our own viability?

Serendipitously, AAC&U (2002) published the National Panel Report, *Greater Expectations: A New Vision for Learning as a Nation Goes to College.* This remarkable document highlighted the problems and solutions facing higher education. This publication assisted Beatty in raising consciousness and instilling passion for engagement with these important issues about learning facing higher education. Our institution had already embarked on reform of the general education requirements, headed by a task force initially cochaired by Page. This task force was under the direction of the dean of the College of Arts and Sciences, as well as a faculty oversight body called the Undergraduate Curricular Forum. Together, we accompanied a cohort of 12 key faculty members to an AAC&U conference on the subject of *Greater Expectations* in March 2003. Thus we were able to capitalize on a powerful motivator: the need to demonstrate to the Board of Trustees that the faculty were the prime movers in the quest for better student outcomes. This task force came to appreciate the interrelatedness of general education assessment, identification of student learning outcomes, national trends in higher education, and our quest for quality within the institution. Further, the conference embraced the concept of meaningful reform within the context of institutional resource constraints. The task force saw examples of programs in peer institutions that were making meaningful improvements without exponentially increasing cost structures. In that brief but heady time, we were convinced and passionate that we could create the type of learning environment envisioned in the *Greater Expectations* document at our very own institution.

So, what happened back at the ranch? There remained some opposition to assessment, especially to the word itself. One particularly eloquent and well respected faculty member begged Beatty at a public forum to "Remember the sanctity of the immeasurable!" Eventually, Beatty was able to call upon the faculty member's discipline of philosophy as the model of assessment. Is this not what philosophers do? This faculty member thought all assessment measures were quantitative in nature and feared a collective disregard for qualitative approaches. This inaccurate assumption led to opposition from one who later became an enthusiastic if skeptical participant in the strategic planning process.

A core cadre of true believers now fully supports and actively pursues meaningful academic reform. Given resource constraints, faculty and administrators are beginning to assign priorities to initiatives that simultaneously meet the needs of teachers, researchers, and students. Students need to learn and retain, faculty should not be overburdened, and administrators need documentation to prove viability. We are convinced that when a reform meaningfully improves the lives of a variety of constituencies, it becomes exciting instead of draining. Examples of this kind of synergy include:

- Student-centered learning activities that generate research and publication opportunities
- Interdisciplinary efforts that generate research and publication opportunities
- Technologies that make assessment, such as the gathering of student learning portfolios, relatively painless for faculty
- Community involvement and feedback that generate career opportunities for students, field research opportunities for faculty, and funding for administrators
- Education reforms that support and make visible the strategic mission and distinctive competence of the institution

Implications

Effective management strategies in higher education are crafted from multiple—even competing—administrative structures and solutions (Ewell, 2004; Rowley & Sherman, 2001). In contrast, management fads inappropriately utilized in higher education are simplistic, universalistic, and overstated—and are therefore at risk for failure (Brindle & Stearns, 2001; Collins, 2000). Fads (e.g., management by objectives, total quality management, business process reengineering, empowerment, and downsizing) become useful models only when they are appropriately linked with other organizational systems and organizational history and offered as food for thought, rather than as the salvation of the organization (Brindle & Stearns, 2001). This linkage takes great skill and perseverance and is very difficult to achieve in higher education.

Higher education organizations are complex and dynamic. Today's solutions are always the cause of tomorrow's problems (Senge, 1994). Institutions of higher education answer to a variety of stakeholders in a strategic context where goals of profitability compete with research priorities, service agendas, and learning outcomes—a level of contradiction, even paradox, that renders any single management intervention relatively ineffective (Rowley & Sherman, 2001). Focusing on any one stakeholder (e.g., trustees, faculty, administration, or students) at the expense of the others can create dysfunction and deficiency (Shinn, 2004). The challenge is magnified due to the problematic alignment of the strategic vision of the leader with the organizational strategies, structures, and cultures present in the institution and the extreme structural inertia working against such alignment. Those who follow the shared governance model learn to respect some fundamental tensions inherent in an inclusive management style:

- Balancing the need for clarity with the reality of complexity and paradox
- Balancing the need for command, consult, and/or consensus leadership styles
- Balancing the inclusion and exclusion of various stakeholders in communication and decision-making processes
- Balancing departmental, discipline-driven perspectives with institutional, strategic mission-driven perspectives
- Balancing strategic planning with iterative implementation

- Balancing a focus on accountability with buffering groups from dysfunctional levels of external pressure and criticism that may result in anger or paralysis

So, what works given the constraints and considering the fact that higher education is a difficult area for effective leadership?

Ironically, balance and the persistence of vision go hand in hand. Cohen (2003) notes that although belief in a powerful vision may be the cause of the opposition, it is also the antidote to it, making the personal pain worth bearing. Cohen also argues that a deep discontent with a lack of vision by bureaucratic bean counters makes most constituencies prefer leadership vision to reactive administration: "Faculty members want to be led (lightly), but not managed" (p. 160). This is a delicate balancing act—how to frame the vision and goals statements so they are concrete and specific enough not to be discounted as meaningless, wandering platitudes, but flexible enough to adapt to the needs of various academic constituencies. Ewell (2004) prefers Dick Cyert's sailboat racing metaphor of keeping the goal in mind but taking advantage of every shift in wind that comes along. Visions should be exciting enough to mobilize collective action, but concerted enough to know which way to steer at each stage.

Notice that this concept of vision is explicitly contextual: leadership in place. Awareness of the context—the wind, the waves, the weather, the crew, the condition of the sails, and the capacity of the boat—makes the difference between success and failure. Beyond management programs, policies, and structures lies a more holistic systems-thinking approach that embraces far more reality than we are normally comfortable dealing with. Kraft (2000) concludes:

> The barriers to . . . excellence in higher education are far deeper than evaluation problems, time

allotments, and the reward system. Research values—cognitive, cerebral, narrowly focused, exclusive, highly deliberate, and solitary—actively work against the values implicit in teaching [and organizational] excellence—those that are intuitive, relational, inclusive, spontaneous, impassioned, and communal. These opposites can be mediated, but only with a sustained and focused effort. Such efforts are rare and sporadic in higher education because they require that we shed our masks and mantles of expertise. . . . that serve as a kind of armor against honest exchanges. Such exchanges appear to be essential to our . . . well-being, to any kind of community, and to genuinely new thoughts and new possibilities. (p. 52)

Through challenging experiences, we have learned that, in the end, technique is not enough. Exciting goals, meaningful visions, brilliant strategic analysis, and contingent action planning—all of these worthy tools are either empowered or rendered powerless by context. For sooner or later, plans go wrong, complexities intrude, unforeseen contingencies arise, and all hell breaks loose. When ambiguity happens, retrospective sensemaking and rationalization run wild. Effective leadership boils down to one essential question: Will the stakeholders around the leader trust the leader to muddle through, because they have faith born of experience that the leader will be fair, look out for them, and not take advantage of them, despite whatever temptations may arise? Or, will they use that moment to attack with all of the contextual weapons that present themselves? If leaders have demonstrated their integrity, developed relationships of trust, and consistently maintained balance and fairness, other stakeholders will often give them the benefit of the doubt. If that foundation is not there, even perfect technique will not be sufficient. This suggests that, to a very real and significant extent, it is the context, not the content, that determines interpretation and meaning. Leadership without a mastery of place becomes impotent, much sound and fury usually resulting in little that will last.

References

Association of American Colleges and Universities. (2002). *Greater expectations: A new vision for learning as a nation goes to college.* Washington, DC: Author.

Avolio, B. J., & Yammarino, F. J. (Eds.). (2002). *Transformational and charismatic leadership: The road ahead.* Danvers, MA: Elsevier Science.

Barker, C. M. (2000). *Liberal arts education for a global society.* New York, NY: Carnegie Corporation of New York.

Beatty, E., Page, R. A., Jr., & Bermudez, H. (2004, January). *Resolving demotivation and misalignment in curricular reform.* Presented at the annual meeting of the Association of American Colleges and Universities, Washington, DC.

Brindle, M. C., & Stearns, P. N. (2001). *Facing up to management faddism: A new look at an old force.* Westport, CT: Quorum Books.

Burns, J. M. (2003). *Transforming leadership: The pursuit of happiness.* New York, NY: Atlantic Monthly Press.

Carnevale, A. P., & Strohl, J. (2001). The demographic window of opportunity: Liberal education in the new century. *Peer Review, 3*(2), 10–13.

Chickering, A. W., & Gamson, Z. F. (Eds.) (2001). *New directions for teaching and learning: No. 47. Applying the seven principles for good practice in undergraduate education.* San Francisco, CA: Jossey-Bass.

Clowes, D. A. (1996). Occupational education. In J. G. Gaff & J. L. Ratcliff (Eds.), *Handbook of the undergraduate curriculum: A comprehensive guide to purposes, structures, practices, and change* (pp. 359–372). San Francisco, CA: Jossey-Bass.

Cohen, A. R. (2003). Transformational change at Babson College: Notes from the firing line. *Academy of Management Learning and Education, 2*(2), 155–180.

Collins, D. (2000). *Management fads and buzzwords: Critical-practical perspective.* New York, NY: Routledge.

Collins, J. (2001). *Good to great: Why some companies make the leap ... and others don't.* New York, NY: HarperCollins.

Cummings, T. G., & Worley, C. (2001). *Organization change and development* (7th ed.). Cincinnati, OH: South-Western College Publishing.

Dixit, A. K., & Nalebuff, B. J. (1991). *Thinking strategically: The competitive edge in business, politics, and everyday life.* New York, NY: W. W. Norton & Company.

Dvir, T., Eden, D., Avolio, B. J., & Shamir, B. (2002). Impact of transformational leadership on follower development and performance. *Academy of Management Journal, 45*(4), 735–744.

Elfin, M. (2003). Longtime observer gives low grade to trends in U.S. higher education. *The Key Reporter, 68*(2), 9–15.

Ewell, P. T. (2004). Management myths. *Change, 36*(1), 4–5.

Finkelstein, M. (2003). The morphing of the American academic profession. *Liberal Education, 89*(4), 6–15.

Fuhrmann, B. S. (1997). Philosophies and aims. In J. G. Gaff & J. L. Ratcliff (Eds.), *Handbook of the undergraduate curriculum: A comprehensive guide to purposes, structures, practices, and change* (pp. 86–99). San Francisco, CA: Jossey-Bass.

Galford, R. M., & Drapeau, A. S. (2002). *The trusted leader: Bringing out the best in your people and your company.* New York, NY: The Free Press.

Kraft, R. G. (2000). Teaching excellence and the inner life of faculty. *Change, 32*(3), 48–52.

Massy, W. F. (2003). *Honoring the trust: Quality and cost containment in higher education.* Bolton, MA: Anker.

Mintzberg, H. (1983). *Power in and around organizations.* Englewood Cliffs, NJ: Prentice Hall.

Moore, T. E. (2003). Transformational change at Babson: Before the first shot was fired. *Academy of Management Learning and Education, 2*(2), 170–72

O'Meara, K., Kaufman, R., & Kuntz, A. M. (2003). Faculty work in challenging times: Trends, consequences, and implications. *Liberal Education, 89*(4), 16–23.

Parker, J. E. (1998). Leading as scholars and educators: The case for collaboration. *The Chronicle of Higher Education, 84*(4), 8.

Pence, J. L. (2003). Dean's dilemmas: Practicing academic leadership. *Liberal Education, 89*(4), 38–45.

Peters, T., & Waterman, R. (1982). *In search of excellence.* New York, NY: Warner Books.

Pfeffer, J. (1972). *Power in organizations.* Boston, MA: Pitman.

Quinn, J. B. (1977). Strategic goals. *Sloan Management Review, 20*(1), 7–22.

Reardon, M. F., & Ramaley, J. (1997). Building academic community while containing costs. In J. G. Goff & J. L. Ratcliff (Eds.), *Handbook of the undergraduate curriculum: A comprehensive guide to purposes, structures, practices, and change* (pp. 513–532). San Francisco, CA: Jossey-Bass.

Rowley, D. J., & Sherman, H. (2001). *From strategy to change: Implementing the plan in higher education.* San Francisco, CA: Jossey-Bass.

Selznick, P. (1957). *Leadership in administration.* New York, NY: Harper & Row.

Senge, P. M. (1990). *The fifth discipline: The art and practice of the learning organization.* New York, NY: Currency Doubleday.

Senge, P. M., Kleiner, A., Roberts, C., Ross, R. B., & Smith, B. J. (1994). *The fifth discipline fieldbook: Strategies and tools for building a learning organization.* New York, NY: Currency Doubleday.

Shin, S. J., & Zhou, J. (2003). Transformational leadership, conservation, and creativity: Evidence from Korea. *Academy of Management Journal, 46*(6), 703–714.

Shinn, L. D. (2004). A conflict of cultures: Governance at liberal arts colleges. *Change, 36*(1), 18–26

Smith, P. (2004). Curricular transformation: Why we need it. How to support it. *Change, 36*(1), 28–35.

Stimpert, J. L. (2004). Turbulent times: Four issues facing liberal arts colleges. *Change, 36*(4), 42–49.

Weick, K. (1979). *The social psychology of organizing* (2nd ed.). Reading, MA: McGraw-Hill.

Wilkins, A. L. (1990). *Cultivating corporate character.* San Francisco, CA: Jossey-Bass.

Zolner, J. (2003). Transformational change at Babson college: A view from the outside. *Academy of Management Learning and Education, 2*(2), 177–180.

11

Conclusion

Jon Wergin

When I introduced the concept of leadership in place at the beginning of this book I didn't offer a definition of what, exactly, I thought it was. That's mostly because, like many others, I had an intuitive feel for what the term meant: a sense that leadership in place is having the opportunity, the ability, and the courage to sense the need for leadership in the moment, then seizing that opportunity. Leaders in place have no expectation that their leadership will lead to long-term changes in their professional roles. They see a need for leadership; they step forward and respond; and then they step back.

As Carol Reineck observes in Chapter 7, "Leadership is difficult to define, but exhilarating to practice." The contributors to this volume have, with their stories, given the exhilaration of leadership in place more grounded definitions by revealing what leaders in place do and how they do it. Their perspectives and opinions are wide and diverse and stem from the places where they have led. Susanne Morgan, Professor X, and Mark Hower and Shana Hormann write with the leadership voices of faculty members; Shelley Chapman and Linda Randall, Victoria Hardy, and Carol Reineck write from the perspective of unit leaders; and Joseph Barwick, Willis Watt, and Ellen Beatty and Robert Page tell their stories from the perspective of those with leadership responsibilities at the institutional level. But despite their differences in institutional setting and professional role, the authors of the previous chapters have told stories that contain remarkably similar lessons. They seem to agree, or nearly so, on what it takes to facilitate leading in place. While the gulf between faculty and administration I described in Chapter 1 is no less real—it certainly exists in some of the tales told here—the breach, it seems, is not one created by widely different values held about who should lead or how they should lead. It's created instead, I submit, by a dual denial: by administrators who are uncomfortable in giving voice to faculty and dealing with the resulting messiness, and by faculty who tell themselves they'd rather not be bothered. What we've tried to provide in this book is a different vision, one articulated beautifully by Joseph Barwick:

> The people who lead from where they are provide the margin between what a college has to be and what it is capable of being. They are followers in that they are following the president, the dean, the department head, or the supervisor. But they are leading in that they are taking those people or processes over which they have authority someplace they would not otherwise go.

Major Themes

The stories in this book suggest that effective leaders in place, whether they hold formal leadership positions or not, do the following:

- They recognize the potential for leadership throughout the institution.
- They build relationships of trust that transcend organizational boundaries.

- They frame problems in ways that challenge conventional thinking while also acknowledging the need to work within the existing structure and culture.
- They are not afraid to take reasonable risks.
- They give voice to a sense of shared purpose and future.
- They exhibit patience and persistence, knowing that real change is neither predictable nor linear.

Effective Leaders in Place Recognize the Potential for Leadership Throughout the Institution

Although Professor X told a compelling story of how *failing* to honor leadership potential led to leadership in place, more constructive approaches exist. Leaders must first make it clear that leadership by others is welcome. As Mark Hower and Shana Hormann suggest, effective academic leaders "create opportunities and experiences for [faculty members] to demonstrate leadership and expertise." Barwick points out that simply recognizing and allowing room for faculty influence isn't nearly enough, however:

> The ability to influence others is a necessary component of leadership, but influencers are not necessarily leaders. Influencers, sometimes called opinion leaders, can shape opinions and sometimes even organizational culture, so they have a great deal of power. However, they typically do not have a sense of direction so much as a position on the issue of the day. Because of their critical thinking and communication skills, they can see ramifications of issues that others might have missed, and thus they can be highly persuasive.

He continues, "True leaders know more than just what they think, believe, or want; they know where they are going (Schein, 1992; Bennis, 1989). Contrary to this is the protester."

Going from influencer or protester to leader can be a big leap, one that faculty may be reluctant to make. As Susanne Morgan points out, faculty members of the Boomer generation may not be clear on what it means to take that step. Back in the 70s, when many now-senior faculty first joined the academy:

> we had to lead against the administration. If we didn't, we were thought to be colluding in oppression and were not trusted by our own peers. This has led, for some of us, to deep confusion about the roles of leaders and the power and authority they may or may not have.
>
> Sometimes it has been hard to take ourselves seriously as leaders and to realize that people look up to us. Even if we understood that we could have brought about the changes we valued by holding official leadership positions, many of us have resisted those positions. It has often been difficult to use the authority we do have, because we have not fully integrated our early beliefs with the demands of formal leadership roles. Some of us have not been as effective leaders as we might have been and have made strategic errors in our leadership.

Further, she writes, "With the sense of not knowing the rules comes a kind of blundering into leadership without internal guidelines about the character of different leadership roles. So we may not be very strategic about leadership in the academy."

Still, as Willis Watt urges, "each one of us must be ready and willing to step up and lead when the time and place are right"—to do what Professor X's colleagues did:

"Different people assumed different kinds of roles, given their backgrounds and positions, in order to lead in place and, in subtle or not so subtle ways, effect change for the better." How do leaders help faculty do that? In *Departments That Work* (2003) I wrote about a concept called *organizational motivation* (a term coined by Barry Staw in the 1980s)—what it takes for members of an organization to set aside at least temporarily their own self-interest in the service of the common good. Effective organizational motivation has two essential ingredients: *identification* and *efficacy*. People must feel, first, as if they are part of an organization that recognizes and values them, and, second, that their service to the organization has a meaningful impact. Reineck recognizes this when she points out that "shared leadership involves creating an environment in which faculty, with their inherent personal strengths, embrace the work of the entire school." Hardy quotes legendary management guru Peter Drucker (1996):

> The motivation of the knowledge worker depends on his being effective, on his being able to achieve. If effectiveness is lacking in his work, his commitment to work and to contribution will soon wither, and he will become a time-server going through the motions from 9 to 5. (p. 4)

Barwick agrees:

> What [faculty] would like to believe, however, is that the work [of the campus] will be different [without them] and that their special contribution to it will be missed. These are the people within the college or university who basically define its character. They are the ones who lead from where they are (Bennis & Nanus, 1985).

Effective Leaders in Place Build Relationships of Trust That Transcend Organizational Boundaries

The tellers of the tales in this book make it clear that effective leadership at any level is all about relationships. This, of course, is nothing new. To say merely that relationships are important in leadership is trite and pedestrian. But the chapter authors have suggested that multiple *kinds* of relationships are important for a leadership-in-place culture to thrive. As Hardy observes, "in times of transitions, it is important to remember that old alliances and new partnerships will merge." Professor X notes that both formal and informal relationships are important: "One of the indications of a strong leadership culture . . . is a healthy flow of communication, through official and unofficial channels, or 'hallway conversations.'" As Morgan reviews her tenure as a leader in place she writes:

> Personal characteristics may be part of the reason that much of my leadership has been largely outside the more formal institutional structure . . . For me, [this] provided a direction for my passion and a way to feel less isolated and more connected in the institution.

Establishing connections among faculty across department boundaries and using these networks to build organizational motivation is a theme that is especially salient in Hower and Hormann's chapter. They write:

> In addition to the expected meetings and retreats of a redesign process, we began a variety of activities to learn about each other. . . . We were discovering what each and all of us did well and valued highly, without concentrating on what was problematic. . . . Our regularly scheduled faculty meetings included time for sharing experiences

related to teaching and learning. We presented high points and struggles, and slowly began to build on one another's expertise.

What did they learn from this?

- "Build and encourage collaborative leadership throughout the organization or unit."
- "Collaborate—even when, maybe especially when—it is not a strength or a widely held practice."
- "Support individual initiative within a context of collective responsibility."
- "Support others when they are leading; take your turn and then let go of the outcome."
- "Be aware and responsible for both tasks and relationships as a shared responsibility, held by each member and the collective team—and not simply by a few authorities."

Those authors writing from positions of formal authority say remarkably similar things about what administrators should do to encourage these kinds of useful relationships. Shelley Chapman and Linda Randall write, "The person in charge . . . will need to divest himself or herself of positional authority and embrace a form of shared leadership with the people." Willis Watt puts it plainly: "It seems apparent to me that effective leadership means creating space for people not in formal authority positions. It also seems obvious to me that effective leaders take the time to develop crucial relationships within the academic community." He continues: "We must empower others to understand who they are and what they hope to achieve—personally and professionally. Empowerment frees people to act." Further:

While we want to motivate others, it is important to be careful to use persuasion that is not based on authority (especially if you are a designated leader), but on a principle of stewardship recognizing that your position of leadership is held at the will of those working beside you. Essentially what I am saying is that empowered leading in place involves people who are aware of and committed to the needs of others. Such empowered leadership is, therefore, better suited to effective and appropriate communication, thereby benefiting individuals and the organization as a whole.

Ellen Beatty and Robert Page urge "a leadership communication style that shares information openly and candidly throughout the organization." Further, they argue, "In an environment where powerful constituencies with competing interests are constantly being tempted to turn communication into an opportunistic weapon, leaders must insist on the free and open sharing of authentic communication and accurate information from everyone involved."

Effective relationships don't develop by themselves. As Hardy points out, "[You have to] build a working relationship independent of agreement or disagreement; you must negotiate the relationship just like any other issue on the table; and you must distinguish how you treat them from how they treat you."

Effective Leaders in Place Frame Problems in Ways That Challenge Conventional Thinking While Also Acknowledging the Need to Work Within the Existing Structure and Culture

Surely one must understand the system and know how to work within it. As Professor X notes in describing the faculty's leadership in place in opposition to an ineffective dean, "we had to follow protocol in order to make it legitimate and safe for us to talk among ourselves and to get all parts of the faculty to listen and to support reform ideas." Leadership in place, however, is not just about working within the system. Effective leaders must understand the culture, knowing almost instinctively what the culture will tolerate; they also must know how to challenge and stretch that culture. Chapman and Randall express this most powerfully in their first leadership principle, "Go deep." By going deep they mean that problems facing leaders are usually not well defined and thus not amenable to pat, superficial solutions:

> Going deep means helping people distinguish between technical problems and adaptive challenges. The typical way to handle a program redesign is for full-time faculty to collaborate on defining the goals of the program and deciding which courses would help students achieve those goals. . . . However, [the department chair] resisted the temptation to make the quick fix and took the risk to embark on a process that would go deeper.

They continue:

> [She] invited [faculty] to come and learn together and to engage in discourse about what their students should learn and how they would learn. . . . [to] shift the focus from how to do things to what meanings they shared with each other about learning and about their discipline.

Because it's uncomfortable, going deep will generally encounter initial resistance. Hardy writes about how difficult it was to bring people together to deal with deep-seated conflicts:

> It was also clear that for a variety of personal and professional reasons, the individual faculty members were not willing to confront either of the two

lead players in this drama. The long-tenured faculty had been working with and around the personnel differences and problems for many years and were tired of the hassle.

Getting the faculty off the dime was reframing the problem in a very direct way: "What is a problem or obstacle that, if solved, would cause an immeasurable change in your life for the better?" Hardy describes the impact of this reframing:

> These two individuals decided that a different form of leadership needed to happen and took responsibility for the next stage of this dilemma. The goal was to significantly change the group so that the work of the program could proceed.

Hower and Hormann reflect similarly, writing about how resistance "includes the withholding and outright fight against anything and everything that constitutes change. Less familiar may be the concept of grace or the embracing of what could be, of a greater possibility." They describe the "greater possibility" this way:

> We had approached the challenge with a technician's sensibilities, so our structural and curricular solutions to the creation of an integrated center were mostly mechanical and cosmetic in nature. . . . [We] first we had to accept that the curriculum needed to fundamentally change. . . . We would need more than our expertise about human and environmental systems, organizational theories, leadership, design, and the like. We would need to change professionally and personally and move into the realm of the unknown into places where we were not always expert and where we could not control the conversation and experi-

ence of change. We would need to embody change itself.

Even with something seemingly straightforward as accreditation self-studies, problem framing is important, as Watt points out:

> I also quickly became aware of the reality that the problems of successfully completing the accreditation process were not all that clear, nor were their solutions clearly defined. A leader who wants to establish a leading-in-place culture must recognize that many problems are not clearly defined with easily identifiable answers.

Effective Leaders in Place Are Not Afraid to Take Reasonable Risks

Hower and Hormann call it "making leaps of faith in good faith." As they looked back on their massive curricular reform, they noted that "small experiments may have been essential for our eventual success." This is part of what Chapman and Randall mean when they write about the importance of going deep: Leaders must "resist the temptation to make the quick fix" and "take the risk to embark on a process that would go deeper," recognizing that, to turn around a cliché made popular by the movie *Apollo 13*, failure *is* an option and can lead to organizational learning. Willingness to take reasonable risks is similar to Reineck's principle of personal courage. In describing the faculty's embrace of program review she writes:

> Committee members showed personal courage when they left their comfort zone and entered into candid discussion with reviewers . . . They had a great personal investment in the product and did not know what the reviewers' comments were

going to be. [But they learned that] the dreaded word "however" can signal the beginning of useful feedback.

Reasonable risk-taking is a major theme in Willis Watt's reflections. "Sadly," he writes, "too often productive change cannot be achieved because, people fear failure. Without our encouragement people are not likely to be willing to take risks . . . So we must develop an environment wherein people feel safe." He continues:

> How does this happen? Leaders must demonstrate to others that taking risks is not only okay, but it is desirable. They should acknowledge that mistakes will be made, but a mistake is not a failure. . . .
>
> Without risk takers the status quo is likely to roll along unhindered, much to the joy of some people in the organization . . . This means that from time to time we must support those willing to break down old structures and practices while putting new ones in their places. Encouraging risk taking means allowing risk taking—to ensure necessary change to achieve organizational success—even the occasional mistake.

Thus, effective leaders in place "emphasize experimentation and creativity in support of key principles and goals," in Hower and Hormann's words.

Effective Leaders in Place Give Voice to a Sense of Shared Purpose and Future

"Without the clarifying and unifying effects of a vivid and compelling vision," write Beatty and Page, "opportunism and turf wars often result in office politics and anarchy (Pence, 2003)." This is certainly true, but as they also point out, "the future is turbulent and uncertain," and thus "can make fools of us all." What distinguishes leadership in place from some other notions of leadership is that the leader's task is not one of dreaming up a vision and then selling it, but one of giving voice to the tacit and implicit visions of others. As Beatty and Page make clear, academic professionals "are energized by articulated, mutually beneficial goals and priorities that give [them] an exciting 'big picture' of the future of the organization and their place in it (Avolio & Yammarino, 2002; Collins, 2001; Galford & Drapeau, 2002; Shin & Zhou, 2003)." Hower and Hormann make essentially the same point: "Articulate and continue to refine a shared vision with the commitment that each member of the faculty needs to have a place for his or her own vision in the larger vision while also supporting the whole." Here the authors are reiterating the key concept of organizational motivation: Energizing work for the good of the whole requires attention to helping people find their organizational niche and also to ensuring that they have a sense of efficacy about their work through mutual interdependence.

As he reflects on his leadership of an accreditation process, Watt notes:

> Through open and honest communication, we realized that we were more than just a work group with a common goal. We shared a common fate. The success of any one of us impacted the success of the others and the achievement of our goal of regional accreditation. Jointly, we agreed that if we were to achieve our specific goal, and ultimately our vision, we could not be just a working group with a common goal, but we must look for win-win outcomes while listening (not just hearing) to each other. Given our common commitment to the college vision, we sought to be responsible for our actions and collaborate with one another.

This sense of collective responsibility for a common goal is what Reineck calls "selfless service." She writes:

> Selfless service among faculty does not result in self-promotion or enhanced personal comfort. While faculty members on the committee gained recognition during and at the conclusion of the process, their motivation was not to gain recognition but rather to serve in an important way and have a significant positive impact on the school to which they were deeply committed.

Collective responsibility goes well beyond a sense of altruism, however. It's much deeper than that: It's a sense of commitment to an organizational culture that has a set of shared values. Sometimes these values are latent and only made tangible when the organization is threatened. Consider this passage from Professor X:

> So, why were we able to develop leadership qualities in what had deteriorated to a rather bad environment, given that leadership qualities typically flourish in a good place? My sense is that it happened because we once had a well functioning organization, and at least tacitly understood our rights and the nature of the framework within which we wanted to operate. To put it differently, we had for a long time worked in a good environment and thus remembered more or less instinctively what that looked like.

A sense of shared purpose and future also does not mean that the collective vision is always congruent with individual, personal visions. Not only is conflict among individual visions normal, it's also healthy, and no organization can grow without it. Barwick suggests that two important qualities of leading in place are "protecting the interests of one group against competing interests of another," and "aligning the interests of one group with those of another." Effective leaders in place thus are able to negotiate inevitable conflicts while also maintaining focus. Beatty and Page write, "Ironically, balance and the persistence of vision go hand in hand . . . Although belief in a powerful vision may be the cause of the opposition, it is also the antidote to it, making the personal pain worth bearing." They argue that "deep discontent with a lack of vision . . . makes most constituencies prefer leadership vision to reactive administration." This leads us to the final principle.

Effective Leaders in Place Exhibit Patience and Persistence, Knowing That Real Change Is Neither Predictable Nor Linear

Most of the contributors to this volume write of struggles to maintain balance between opposing forces:

- Between disequilibrium and adaptation (Chapman and Randall)
- Between reality and possibility (Beatty and Page)
- Between tradition and change (Hower and Hormann)
- Between personal needs and political realities (Professor X)
- Between seeing oneself as an outsider and as an insider (Morgan)
- Between commitment to personal gain and the general welfare (Watt)

Effective leaders in place are patient enough to know that real change takes time and requires adaptation to changing circumstances; they also are sufficiently committed to change that they are willing to see it through. Chapman and Randall are most explicit about this point: Their first principle, "go deep," is followed by "be patient with distress," "attend to needs," "monitor the process," and "regard progress." Their analysis of all of these points merits studying in detail, as it's full of wise advice. Referring to "regard progress" they write:

> The chairperson needed to put herself in and out of the process, repeatedly. She needed to be in the process enough to gauge and guide, but out of the process enough to assure it would be the people who did the work, that their interests would be represented, and their decisions would be made. She also had to make sure that the . . . faculty did not lapse into technical problem solving when the adaptive challenge seemed tough. One member of the group initially wanted to fall back on old ways of doing things . . . The chairperson and center staff gently led him to value the process as a group effort that would yield new and adaptive solutions.

Effective leaders, they're saying, are able to engage the group and create disequilibrium that is just enough to stretch people beyond their "comfort zone" (in Reineck's words).

Beatty and Page write about the same phenomenon by coming at it from the other extreme—they caution that while people can be excited by possibilities, they need to be prepared for discomfort:

> Exciting goals, meaningful visions, brilliant strategic analysis, contingent action planning—all of these worthy tools are either empowered or rendered powerless by context. For sooner or later, plans go wrong, complexities intrude, unforeseen contingencies arise, and all hell breaks loose. When ambiguity happens, retrospective sensemaking and rationalization run wild.

Thus, they argue, one of the most difficult leadership tasks is the ability to read the situation and judge just how much stress the group can handle. They continue:

> If leaders have demonstrated their integrity, developed relationships of trust, and consistently maintained balance and fairness, other stakeholders will often give them the benefit of the doubt. If that foundation is not there, even perfect technique will not be sufficient. This suggests that, to a very real and significant extent, it is the context, not the content, that determines interpretation and meaning. Leadership without a mastery of place becomes impotent, much sound and fury usually resulting in little that will last.

Hower and Hormann write that leaders should "accept that change includes the unknown and that managing anxiety about ambiguity is essential as a personal and collective practice." Remain open to new possibilities, they urge. Focus attention on principles and what is working, rather than on the details of what is wrong.

Professor X found that persistence requires stepping back periodically and regrouping:

> Leading from the core for me meant that I needed to find a balance among my concerns for the institution, being politically active, and making sure I refueled to maintain the drive and energy to keep going. That drive, interestingly enough, came directly from my passion for what I do. What is often touted as being in opposition to faculty collaboration—namely faculty individualism—grounded me during turbulent times.

Being patient and persistent pays off, as Susanne Morgan reflects upon her 30-plus years as a leader in place:

But in the end we have indeed been leaders, and our generation has indeed transformed college teaching. We were part of the shift that moved students into the picture of academic work and even closer to the center. We were leaders in our departments as we tried to establish the systematic use of student evaluations in assessment of teaching. Some of us even campaigned for student participation in departmental discussions of curriculum and even of personnel issues.

We led by being what is now called scholarly teachers: We read *Radical Teacher* and the fledgling periodicals on teaching in our disciplines and in higher education. Some of us led by organizing colleagues and persisting until our institutions formed and supported centers for teaching. . . .

After bitterly decrying the values and orientation of our disciplines, we have seen them incorporate much of what we stood for.

Two key insights spring from this passage. First, Morgan is describing how she and her colleagues, without even knowing it, engaged in leadership that made a difference. By pecking away at stubborn institutional practice, they were able to create transformative change. Second, it's clear that what sustained their efforts was a commitment to a core set of values, in Morgan's case centering on the importance of the college's teaching mission. This latter point is one that Willis Watt returns to again and again. "Leading in place," he writes, "means you must sometimes do the right thing and stand by your decision and actions in order to ensure the larger good of the organization."

But how does one do that? How does one know when to adjust to the demands of the moment—to be sensitive to the context that Beatty and Page stress so highly—and when to hold firm to principle?

Part of the answer, I believe, lies in the concept of *voice,* which, thanks to Stephen Covey, has been revived in a new way. In his book, *The Eighth Habit,* Covey (2004) writes that the central challenge of leadership—the eighth habit—is to "find your voice and inspire others to find theirs" (p. 5). Clearly, leaders in place first have to find their voice, a compelling reason for stepping forward and becoming a leader. As Covey put it, "When you engage in work that taps your talent and fuels your passion—that rises out of a great need in the world that you feel drawn by conscience to meet—therein lies your voice, your calling, your soul's code" (p. 5).

Finding—or not finding—voice played a key role in each of the leadership stories contained in this book. Morgan and her colleagues had a sense of calling throughout their careers. Professor X was able to maintain the voice of a faculty member while also finding a leadership voice. Hardy's warring faculty members struggled, partly because their talent and passion were not matched by conscience and need, in stark contrast to Hower and Hormann, who saw a way to respond to a critical institutional challenge by doing the right thing in a way that made best use of their talent and passion. Randall (of Chapman and Randall) saw her calling as one of reinventing her department, drawing upon the energy of part-time faculty. Reineck found her voice in the leadership principles she brought with her from the military. Barwick, Watt, and Beatty and Page have all found their voice in being institutional leaders.

But leadership in place, whether someone is a formal leader or not, requires a commitment to helping others find *their* voices as well. This is what is missing in Barwick's influencer or protester. One can speak from passion and experience, with the firm belief that motives are honorable and that the message needs to be heard and still not be a leader in place. One can sound off at a faculty meeting about the latest administrative incursion into faculty autonomy and then retire to the sanctity of a private office with the smug satisfaction that comes from being a voice in the wilderness. Or that same person can do what Professor X did (or, less dramatically, what Morgan, Hower and Hormann, Randall, and other leaders in place did), which is to commit to something much riskier—helping others find their voices in a common cause.

Leadership in Place: Challenges Ahead

In Chapter 1, I wrote about how the predominant models of academic organization, especially the isolation of individual faculty members brought on by their highly specialized work, have produced a managerial culture that inhibits a sense of collective responsibility to the institution. I suggested a return to a neocollegial model of faculty work in which academic professionals participate more effectively in the life of the campus and introduced the notion of *leadership in place* as a needed antidote to the toxic gulf between faculty and administration that the managerial culture has produced.

The contributors to this book have demonstrated how leadership in place works and how it *can* work. They have also demonstrated how difficult leadership in place can be in the current academic culture. To be sure, leadership in place exists throughout the academy in spite of the cultural barriers. Academic professionals everywhere are finding their voice and inspiring others to find theirs. What is needed, however, is a setting where leadership in place is more the rule than the exception and where leadership is everybody's business—a setting that is more accommodating of the forces for change I mentioned in Chapter 1. Creating a more congenial academic organization for leadership in place will, like leadership in place itself, require courage and persistence. Some of the key challenges follow.

A Hostile or Apathetic System of Academic Governance

An academy with broader and more genuinely shared leadership will require that academic governance change as well. The traditionally creaky forms of academic governance have been unable to keep the lid on the "organized anarchy" of the academy for at least the past quarter century. Three ingredients of successful governance—participation, responsiveness, and efficiency—have all declined since the mid-1970s because of an increasingly fragmented culture, a steadily increasing external presence, and more corporate-like administrative approaches (Slaughter, Kittay, & Duguid, 2001). A new governance strategy must leave behind a focus on convenience and control by the administration on one hand and individual entrepreneurship by the faculty at the expense of institutional citizenship on the other. The new academy will require a renewed form of shared governance based on collective responsibility, a system that blends individual with mutual accountability.

Separation of the Learning Mission From the Governance Mission

As the chapters in this book have amply demonstrated, academic leadership is not what happens when designated administrators try to figure out how to foist some initiative or other on a mostly unwilling faculty. Instead, leadership should occur at all levels of the organization, and the role of designated leaders should be to assist the community in making important choices. In the first empirically grounded study of transformative change in higher education (Kezar & Eckel, 2002), the researchers made a remarkable discovery. They found that institutions able to make deep and lasting changes created an environment where "sensemaking activities" could occur. They defined *sensemaking* as follows:

Sensemaking is the reciprocal process where people seek information, assign it meaning, and act. It is the collective process of structuring meaningful sense out of uncertain and ambiguous organizational situations. Sensemaking allows people to craft, understand, and accept new conceptualizations of the organization and then to act in ways consistent with those new interpretations. (p. 314).

An Imbalance of Organizational Tensions

In her book *Changing Academic Work,* Elaine Martin (1999) points to four tensions likely to be at the center of the new academy—individuality versus collaboration, vision versus reality, reward versus accountability, and valuing the past versus being open to the future. (Note how similar these are to the tensions identified by our chapter authors.) She urges that our goal should not be to resolve these tensions but to manage them in ways that will keep them in balance:

Collaboration needs robust individualism to work; visions cannot work unless they are informed by the reality of day-to-day experience; reward becomes facile unless charged with accountability; and the virtue of the past can only remain enchanting when balanced against the demands of the future . . . *The essential task which we as academic staff face in doing this balancing is a learning task.* (p. 148, italics added)

And finally, the most daunting challenge to leadership in place is presented by the potential leaders in place themselves. Getting faculty members and other academic professionals to gain a sense of efficacy and to believe that they really are in a position to make a difference will require attention to a cultural inertia that has been years in the making.

References

Covey, S. R. (2004). *The eighth habit: From effectiveness to greatness*. New York, NY: The Free Press.

Drucker, P. F. (1966). *The effective executive*. New York, NY: HarperCollins.

Kezar, A., & Eckel, P. (2002, June). Examining the institutional transformation process: The importance of sensemaking, interrelated strategies, and balance. *Research in Higher Education, 43*(3), 295–328.

Martin, E. (1999). *Changing academic work: Developing the learning university*. Philadelphia, PA: Open University Press.

Slaughter, S., Kittay, J., & Duguid, P. (2001, Spring). Technology, markets, and the new political economy of higher education. *Liberal Education, 87*(2) 6–17.

Wergin, J. F. (2003). *Departments that work: Building and sustaining cultures of excellence in academic programs*. Bolton, MA: Anker.

Name Index

Subject Index